AMERICAN WRITING SINCE 1945

AMERICAN WRITING SINCE 1945
A Critical Survey

Robert F. Kiernan

FREDERICK UNGAR PUBLISHING CO.
New York

Copyright © 1983 by Frederick Ungar Publishing Co., Inc.

Printed in the United States of America

Design by Anita Duncan

Library of Congress Cataloging in Publication Data

Kiernan, Robert F.
    American writing since 1945.

    Bibliography: p.
    Includes index.
    1. American literature—20th century—History and
criticism.   I. Title.
PS225.K48   1983   810'.9'0054   83-828
ISBN 0-8044-2458-6
ISBN 0-8044-6359-X (pbk.)

For Lynn and Steve, Brian and Scott

PREFACE

"If you cannot believe in the greatness of your own age and inheritance," Shaw once wrote to Ellen Terry, "you will fall into confusion of mind and contrariety of spirit." My students seem to feel that contemporary American literature engenders its own "confusion of mind and contrariety of spirit," but, without wishing to sound as threatening as Shaw, I agree with him that contemporary literature is at least as important as established literature in its gifts to our sensibilities. It is, after all, *our* literature, and it speaks to us in ways that no readers generations hence will experience as gainfully as we, no matter how learned they may be about our curious age.

My attitude was not always thus. In younger days, daunted by the unstoppable flow of our literature, I resolved to read nothing that had not survived in bookstalls for at least fifty years—to let time winnow contemporary literature to manageable proportions. I am convinced now that we impoverish ourselves by focusing narrowly on "great" authors rather than on the full, rich flow of literature. Consequently, I have chosen in the following pages to place less emphasis on major writers than would ordinarily be accorded them. I do this not because I would challenge the eminence of the Saul Bellows and the Robert Lowells, but because I would give equal attention to the near-greats who stand in their shadows.

I conceive of this book, then, as a modest introduction to the wealth of American literature written since World War II. The work of some three hundred novelists, playwrights, and

Preface

poets is chronicled, and I have tried to suggest the appeal of individual writers as well as of schools of writers. It seems to me inappropriate to depart radically from general opinion in a work of this sort. I owe an acknowledgment, therefore, to critical writing in the field, which I have ransacked gratefully for nomenclature and for understanding. For the occasional sentence and phrase, I have also plundered my own articles on American literature and on individual writers in Ungar's *Encyclopedia of World Literature in the 20th Century* (rev. ed., 1981 ff.).

Many friends and colleagues have helped to shape this study. I am especially grateful to Manhattan College professors Mary Ann O'Donnell and John Nagle, who read the entire manuscript and suggested many improvements. I am grateful also to Professor Paul Cortissoz, who read the chapter on drama; to the librarians of the Manhattan College Library, the New York Public Library, and the Schomberg Center for Research in Black Culture, who were indefatigably kind; to Leonard Klein, senior editor at Frederick Ungar, who proposed this project and saw it to completion; and to Professor Ernest Speranza, who proofread the manuscript. I am grateful finally to Manhattan College for a sabbatical leave during which the text was written.

R.F.K.

New York, N.Y.
June 1982

CONTENTS

x   Contents

1 · THE BACKGROUND

One of the most dubious conventions of literary thought is the use of historical categories—the Age of Chaucer, for instance, and the Victorian Period. Such tags are conventions of discourse, certainly, but are more riddled with contradictions than we generally admit, and their contradictions tend to erupt eccentrically, as if coiled springs, to discomfort the Procrusteans who would lie easily with history. In this survey of contemporary American writing, therefore, I make no pretense of delimiting a literary period. Were periodization my impulse, I would probably link the literature to modernism and ultimately to the octopus embrace of Romanticism, but there seems to me little value in such grand-scale pushing and shoving. The contemporary period of American literature compels attention because its life and breath are ours; it will command attention in the future, I am certain, because writers such as Vladimir Nabokov, Denise Levertov, and Sam Shepard will not easily escape the attention of posterity. But I cannot think that the period 1945 to 1982 will ever be viewed as a monolith, neatly circumscribed and of unified character.

The literary amorphousness of the period is largely a reflection of the national life. Political, intellectual, and cultural developments have tended to texture the postwar years without lending them notable shape or direction, and since the end of World War II each decade in America has seen an abrupt and startling change in the national ethos. The literary imagination has marched in step with this cultural disarray and has even seized upon a myth. As Hercules is a touchstone figure for the Enlightenment, Prometheus for the Romantics, and Ulysses for the period that stretches from Tennyson to Joyce, it is Proteus, the fabulous shape-changer, who epitomizes the spirit of the postwar years and who recurs most frequently in its literature.

American political life has been especially changeable. Because America emerged from World War II the dominant world power, its factories unbombed and its technology triumphant, one might have expected a cultural breakdown similar to that which followed World War I—a loosening of wartime corsets, as it were, and a resumption of the independent spirit. But the conviction that a cold war existed between the Soviet Union and the United States gained immediate currency in the postwar years, especially in America, and the socialist nations of Eastern Europe were thought to be aligned on one side of a battle for global domination, the so-called free nations of the world on the other. "They" were totalitarian and godless, "we" were free—so went the simple dialectic. Yet the immediate consequence of America's assuming leadership of the free bloc of nations was the growth of a deeply conformist spirit. As much a uniform as khaki-colored wool, the ubiquitous gray-flannel suit became the symbol of the fifties, and witch hunts, blacklists, and loyalty oaths supplanted the radical politics and Marxist dabbling of the prewar years. Senator Joseph McCarthy and the House Committee on Un-American Activities made it clear that to question any aspect of the American way was tantamount to disloyalty, and the net effect of this mentality was to make recognition of the racial prejudice and class privilege that strained the country's social fabric all but impossible. The cold-war mentality of the 1950s only gave way under the pressure of a 1960s activism directly traceable to such ostrichism. The campus antiwar movements, black assertiveness, hippie and other countercultural movements, the efforts to create a "poor people's movement"—all were an explosion in the 1960s of social tensions ignored during the conformist fifties. In the perspective of time, all seem now to have been cultural explosions as much as political movements, their result not only a greater awareness of racial minorities and the poor, but a reestablishment of America's historical tolerance for political and social deviance.

Indeed, the 1950s notion that Americans were a homogenous people was entirely shattered in the 1960s as radical social criticism asserted itself and as intellectuals reassumed their traditionally dissident stance with respect to the institutions that had assimilated them during the Eisenhower and Kennedy years. It was almost as if the cultural breakdown one looked for after World War II had simply been postponed. The assassinations of President Kennedy, Senator Robert Kennedy, and the black leader Martin Luther King seemed evidence that something was deeply amiss in American life, and the enormously unpopular Vietnam war and the scandals of the Nixon presidency served further to disenchant large numbers of Americans, especially the educated and the young. The besieged-garrison mentality of the 1950s was supplanted by a prevailing sense that the enemies were within the gates—not because they had breached the walls, but because they were born citizens.

Soaring monetary inflation and increasing unemployment in the 1970s caused the national interest to refocus once again, just as abruptly as before. A Middle Eastern oil cartel began seriously to undermine America's economy in 1971, and a mood of individual self-preservation swept over the country, superseding such altruistic concerns of the sixties as the ecosystem, governmental integrity, and the political enfranchisement of minorities. The young began to prepare more seriously to enter the work force, and workers nervously watched their savings erode. Britain's lost status seemed to portend America's eclipse, and a new conservatism dramatically announced itself in 1980 with the election of Ronald Reagan to the presidency. From the wartime forties, then, to the patriotic conformity of the fifties, to the strident radicalism of the sixties, to the conservatism of the seventies: the American ethos, like Proteus, proved impossibly various.

The religious life of the nation was an interesting barometer of this variety. A revivalist spirit reigned in the 1950s, and religious leaders like Norman Vincent Peale, Fulton J. Sheen, and Billy Graham enjoyed enormous success by equating moral righteousness with the American way of life. A distaste for their kind of piety set in during the 1960s, however, partly in response to Dietrich Bonhoeffer's emphasis on the need for a secular interpretation of the Scriptures and partly in response to neoorthodox Protestant theology, with its emphasis on human loneliness and vulnerability—the need, in Paul Tillich's phrase, for "the courage to be." If the 1950s were pietistic, the 1960s and early 1970s were militant: numerous churchmen and -women took up the cry against the Vietnam war and participated actively in demonstrations for racial equality, and their countercultural gospel came to prevail over more conservative religious voices. Radical theologies seemed to spring up overnight, challenging dogma and traditional church practices, and interest in Eastern religions and cults seemed to increase geometrically as membership in the traditional churches plummeted. Like secular leaders during these tumultuous years, religious leaders vacillated in their tolerance of dissident behavior, uncertain where they themselves stood, and uncertain how to align their institutions with the future. But once again the temper of the country changed abruptly: with the new conservatism of the late 1970s and early 1980s, pietism revived to some limited extent, and Jerry Falwell's "Moral Majority" crusade began to unravel freedoms assembled at great human cost in the preceding decades.

Intellectual life in the age was hardly more coherent. More than any other group, sociologists impressed their discipline on the public mind in the postwar years, and they were generally critical of mass society, as in David Riesman's influential treatise *The Lonely Crowd* (1950) and in C. Wright Mills's *The Power Elite* (1956). Yet while sociologists like Riesman and Mills probed the large-scale determinants of American behavior, another school of sociological thought, best represented by the works of Erving Goffman, subordinated that focus to the study of minute dramaturgies of adjustment, such as facial expression and body posture. Together, the two schools tended to fracture sociological methodology and understanding.

A clash between behaviorists and Freudians divided the intellectual community in a similar way. On one hand, the behaviorist B. F. Skinner insisted that human conduct should be understood as a complex of reactions to established stimuli or signals; his belief that self-awareness and insight may be detrimental to effective behavior was one of the great visions of the period, challengingly set forth in his *Beyond Freedom and Dignity* (1971). On the other hand, the Freudian belief that effective behavior is the fruit of insight, self-knowledge, and ego identification continued to dominate psychoanalytical thought, notably in the voluminous writings of Erik Erikson, whose early *Childhood and Society* (1950) has been enormously influential, and also in Robert Coles's multivolume *Children of Crisis* (1967). Statistical studies contributed to the general confusion by pitting massive, dispassionate surveys against widespread assumptions about American life. Alfred Kinsey's *Sexual Behavior in the Human Male* (1948) and *Sexual Behavior in the Human Female* (1953) were the most startling of these. Further complicating the age's understanding of human behavior, the British anti-Freudian R. D. Laing argued that insanity may be a healthy response to a mad world, and his argument glossed antiestablishment behavior in the Vietnam years to a degree that many found unsettling.

A number of post-Freudian social critics challenged the age with radical analyses of its mores and disquieting calls for psychic liberation. With Nazi Germany a portentous example, the immigrant intellectuals Wilhelm Reich and Herbert Marcuse argued that psychic structures tend to take their form from social structures, and they viewed with alarm certain echoes of authoritarian class structure in the contemporary American psyche. Reich called for the emancipation of libidinal energy as a way of changing this authoritative disposition; Marcuse, in such influential works as *Eros and Civilization* (1955) and *One Dimensional Man* (1964), called more specifically for a liberation of erotic and aesthetic consciousness. The ideas of Reich and Marcuse were echoed in the writings of Paul Goodman and Norman O. Brown. Goodman's *Growing Up Absurd* (1960) drew sympathetic attention to the dropout and Beat cultures of the 1950s, and his earlier *Communitas* (1947) helped in the late 1960s to inspire interest in establishing utopian communities. Brown's *Life against Death* (1959) and *Love's Body* (1966) complement Goodman's writing in arguing that culture and civilization are inexorably alien to human fulfillment. A holistic eroticism is humanity's only salvation, Brown insisted, and like all of these social critics, he cultivated a prophetic tone and an apocalyptic rhetoric that touched many Americans deeply.

Science and technology also tended to disorient and disquiet the age. Nuclear power, computers, moon landings, the identification of DNA, astrophysical discoveries such as quasars, radio galaxies, and black holes: all seemed science-fiction fantasy become real, and in many quarters such developments instilled a heady feeling of progress. Yet a troubling sense that science and technology are cancerous growths in the human community also took hold, not only because developments in physics, cybernetics, and technology outstripped the culture's ability to deal with their moral and social implications, but because some of the developments seemed to threaten Armageddon, particularly the risks of nuclear warfare and irreversible damage to the ecosystem. Another area of concern has been the tendency of science and technology to enthrone artificial intelligence, for a mechanization of thought and information has come to dominate creativity in recent decades, notably so with the spread of computer usage. Humans seem fated to end their tenure on earth as technicians—as sophisticated custodians of machines more sophisticated than they.

But once again the cultural stance is not coherent. The social philosopher Lewis Mumford was eloquent in his mistrust of outsize technology, especially in *The Myth of the Machine* (1967) and *The Pentagon of Power* (1970), and the French sociologist Jacques Ellul was influentially fatalistic about what he called "the calculus of efficiency" in his treatise *The Technological Society* (1964). Yet technologists themselves have reveled in the world of machines. The inventive R. Buckminster Fuller was deeply committed to the technological principle that more is accomplished with less, and his utopian vision of the technological future, expounded in numerous books and lectures, gained him a considerable following in the sixties and seventies. In a more humanistic vein, Marshall McLuhan argued in his *Understanding Media* (1964) that the world had been "retribalized" by modern communication systems—that a "global village" had recaptured through technology the intimate scale of life generally thought destroyed by technology. The mathematician Norbert Wiener even devoted himself to the social and ethical questions raised by cybernetics and to the overlapping interests of cybernetics and religion in *The Human Use of Human Beings* (1950) and *God and Golem, Inc.* (1964). Both the technological enthusiasts and the antitechnologists have had their influential spokesmen, who are by no means simplistically polarized. The culture is not so much divided by their points of view as it is agitated.

The life of literature in the postwar years has been deeply touched by this cultural disarray, although not always in a simple or predictable manner. On one hand, regional literature flourished with surprising vigor in the 1950s, when a homogenized America seemed the national ideal; and as society assumed an increasingly urban character in that decade, Southern writers stubbornly celebrated a rural and traditionalist sensibility. Jewish and black writers also set their characters in opposition to the urban environment. On the other hand, as the Vietnam involvement turned increasingly sour, writers largely rejected familiar forms: the well-made play that was Broadway's staple offering, the lyrical-realistic narrative brought to eminence by Fitzgerald and Hemingway, the formalist verse enthroned by academia's New Critics. Writers came to think these expressions of the literary mind too lucid for the period's darkness, and they devoted themselves instead to a literature of tortuous sensibility. Solipsism and madness were often their chosen terrain. In a more simple line of influence, writers like Flannery O'Connor and Robert Lowell reflected the variant religious interests of the age, while writers like Thomas Pynchon and Norman Mailer embraced its burgeoning technology. John Barth and Donald Barthelme seized upon the new media consciousness, and schools of black and feminist literature were inspired by the Black Power and feminist movements. In short, the relationship between literature and its host culture was what it always is—obvious, devious, inescapable, complex. The literature itself was as successful and as unsuccessful as its age, and just as diverse.

2 · FICTION

Unlike those writers who survived World War I, the novelists and short-story writers who came to prominence immediately after World War II had little sense of a world born afresh. They were not inclined, therefore, like the writers of the twenties, to compose radical manifestos. Neither did they proclaim brashly a necessity at all costs to "make it new." They generally behaved as if the prewar conventions of fiction were still viable and as if the continuity of American literature were unbroken. Norman Mailer was typical of them, worrying about who would write the new *Farewell to Arms*, and preparing himself to assume Ernest Hemingway's (1899–1961) crown by studying Joseph Warren Beach's *American Fiction, 1920–1940* (1941) as if it were a training manual. A considerable part of Mailer's problem was that the continuity of American literature *was* unbroken. Hemingway himself was still on the scene, belligerent and monolithic, his every move emblazoned on the covers of *Life* magazine. If *Across the River and into the Trees* (1950) suggested Hemingway was losing his touch, *The Old Man and the Sea* (1952) was awesome in both form and technique—a caution to anyone who would seize the laurels before Hemingway's demise. John Dos Passos (1896–1970), another novelist of the First World War, was also still prolific, publishing nineteen works in the years between 1945 and 1966. William Faulkner too was still publishing, and the outpouring of the second Yoknapatawpha cycle between 1951 and 1962 confirmed his vigor.

9

NATURALISTS AND REALISTS

Most writers who had established their reputations before World War II simply continued after the war to write in the naturalistic and realistic manner that had brought them to fame. James T. Farrell (1904–1979), Sinclair Lewis (1885–1951), John O'Hara (1905–1970), James Gould Cozzens (1903–1978), and John Steinbeck (1902–1968) all persisted in emphasizing heredity, environment, and humanity's elemental nature. They persisted, too, in grounding their fictions in realistic detail, permanently compounding realism and naturalism. If critics of the novel just as persistently announced the death of such fiction, it was because the postwar efforts of these novelists had a less cutting edge than their prewar efforts. Farrell's *Bernard Clare* (1946), *The Silence of History* (1963), and *What Time Collects* (1964) are not so effectively pitiless as his Studs Lonigan trilogy, and Lewis's *Cass Timberlane* (1945), *Kingsblood Royal* (1947), *The God-Seeker* (1949), and *World So Wide* (1951) seemed perfumed with formaldehyde even as they arrived at the bookstalls. O'Hara continued to anatomize the hidden life of his Lantenengo County as if it were Faulkner's Yoknapatawpha, but such novels as *A Rage to Live* (1949), *Ten North Frederick* (1955), and *Ourselves to Know* (1960) are irredeemably slick, their emotional understanding too little, their naturalistic logic too encompassing. In trying to take the measure of America, these novelists also moralized vastly. Whatever its original integrity, naturalism tended to become in their postwar novels a philosophy of empty gesture and shrill rhetoric.

Because of the profound impact of biological studies on his fiction, John Steinbeck must be numbered among the postwar writers who continued in the naturalistic tradition. Steinbeck tended to compound his biology with mysticism, however, and in much of his postwar fiction the result is a glow of optimism quite at odds with naturalistic pessimism. Naked biology animates Mack and the boys in *Cannery Row* (1945) and the Hawley family in *The Winter of Our Discontent* (1961), but evil in these novels is only the frustration of atavistic impulses, and salvation is always as close as shantytown. So radical is this simplification that Steinbeck's postwar fictions seem to exemplify a mythic consciousness as much as naturalistic thought.

Like Steinbeck, James Gould Cozzens shares a basic philosophy with the naturalists. Circumstances, environment, a proneness to error, a capacity for evil—all limit human freedom in his postwar novels *Guard of Honor* (1948), *By Love Possessed* (1957), and *Morning Noon and Night* (1968). But Cozzens is less interested in the underbelly of social life than in exploring just how freely human beings can deal with moral anarchy. Unlike most naturalists, he invents characters of refined sensibility, like Abner Coates, Julius Penrose, and Arthur Winner, Jr.—doctors, lawyers, generals, divines. Because they see a need to constrain moral anarchy, they generally endorse the established social orders. Cozzens has been widely attacked for this cultural conservatism, and critics tend to see him as an errant naturalist. He is more properly understood as a novelist of manners.

The influence of Hemingway is discernible in a conviction among many contemporary novelists that the writer is a public figure, free to court acclaim by parading his individuality, and privileged to elevate his vocation to the rank of public symbol. James Jones (1921–1977), Nelson Algren (b. 1909), Gore Vidal (b. 1925), and Norman Mailer (b. 1923) do not in any sense comprise a Hemingway school, but each has cultivated public notoriety, and each has invoked a nostalgia for individual heroics that nicely compounds with a show of individuality. The public persona is for each a calculated extension of his art. A younger generation of realists, best represented by John Gardner (1933–1982) and Robert Stone (b. 1937), is less prone to such theatrics.

James Jones's career is dominated by his first work, *From Here to Eternity* (1951). Powerfully realistic in its depiction of army life in the months preceding Pearl Harbor, the novel is compelling in its view of a naturalistic world that the hero can

neither "stomach nor understand nor explain nor change."
From Here to Eternity lacks both subtlety and mature technique, however, largely because Jones thought himself a born
writer with a duty to remain unschooled in the finer points of
craftsmanship. *The Pistol* (1959), *The Thin Red Line* (1962),
and the posthumous *Whistle* (1978) are also realistic novels
about army life and on that basis superior to *Some Came Running* (1958) and *In the Merry Month of May* (1971), novels
blighted even more than Jones's war novels by fuzzy philosophizing and discordant syntax. The ultimate appeal of Jones's
fiction depends on a carefully merchandised sense that the author, like Hemingway, "was there."

Nelson Algren brings a very different talent to the naturalist legacy but with no less insistent a claim for the authority
of his sensibility. *The Man with the Golden Arm* (1949), his
best novel, is unimpeachably gritty in its South Side of Chicago
setting, and Algren is nicely bemused by his characters' skid-
row vernaculars, if poetically anguished over the doom that
awaits them. Algren's parade of his sensibility is somewhat
brash, however, for his juggling of the naturalistic, the mock
epical, and the romantically melancholic fails to convince us
that his Chicagoans are archetypes and that Algren's feeling
for them should be the pattern for our own. In *A Walk on the
Wild Side* (1956), Algren's softhearted thugs even seem kin to
Damon Runyon's golden-hearted prostitutes, and the likeness
points up a sentimental quicksand on which Algren's fictions
are built. A measure of irony or emotional restraint might have
served him well as bedrock.

Gore Vidal's fictions range from the war novel *Williwaw*
(1946) to the historical novels *Julian* (1964), *Burr* (1973), and
Creation (1981), to the high camp extravaganzas *Myra Breckinridge* (1968) and *Myron* (1974). There is something ventril-
oquistic about Vidal's talent, as this range suggests. Because
plotting is not his strength, he tends to affect an array of voices:
dry wit for his Aaron Burr, overripe hyperbole for his Myra
Breckinridge, world-weariness for his Emperor Julian. His favorite narrative form is the make-believe journal, no doubt

because it obviates the need for elaborate plot and showcases his mimetic ability.

Vidal's weightiest fictions are his historical novels, which are solidly researched and interestingly iconoclastic. His masterworks, however, are the Hollywood novels *Myra Breckinridge* and *Myron*, which trace the career of the transsexual Myra Breckinridge as she tries to save Hollywood's tackiest films, even Hollywood itself, from oblivion. Like Burr, Myra is utterly irrepressible and majestically out of step with the world. She is a marvelous confection, one of the great characters of contemporary fiction. Vidal's reputation as a serious novelist has unfortunately suffered from the lightness of her story, as if he himself were Myra Breckinridge and as if lightness of touch were lightness of mind.

Norman Mailer, by contrast, is a highly successful entrepreneur who has parlayed exhibitionist behavior into an implausible literary eminence. He came to prominence with his first novel, *The Naked and the Dead* (1948). An impressive study of war but much more than a war novel, it is the story of an infantry platoon that pits itself against enemy forces on a small, Japanese-held island in the South Pacific and pits itself in a larger sense against the deterministic universe. In its wake, the novels *Barbary Shore* (1951), *The Deer Park* (1955), and *An American Dream* (1965) seem thin and barely competent. *Why Are We in Vietnam?* (1967), however, is arguably superior to *The Naked and the Dead* and clear evidence that the success of that novel was not fortuitous. An energetic narrative written in the jazzy patois of a disc jockey, it is, once again, something more than a war novel.

In recent decades, Mailer's energies have generally turned from the novel to nonfiction, and such works as *Advertisements for Myself* (1959), *The Armies of the Night* (1968), *The Prisoner of Sex* (1971), *Marilyn: A Biography* (1973), and *The Executioner's Song* (1979) have established his reputation as a heavyweight journalist. Because he employs novelistic skills in writing them, Mailer thinks of his journalistic endeavors as "nonfiction novels." Whatever their proper genre, many of his "nonfiction novels" are journalistically daunting. Their narrative vitality is enormous; their ideological contentions are profound, and they have on occasion shaped our understanding of the historical moment. Their success is due in large part to an auctorial candor that salts Mailer's rhetoric. *The Armies of the Night* is an account of a march on the Pentagon in October 1967, and it includes an account of Mailer's deliberate provocation of federal marshals so that a filmmaker might photograph him being led off to jail. Once incarcerated, Mailer worries inanely whether he will be released in time to attend a fashionable party that "has every promise of being wicked, tasty, and rich."

But doubts persist about the durability of Mailer's journalistic writings. Their cogency is increasingly dependent on the reader's knowledge that "all this really happened" and that the "I" of the nonfiction really is Mailer. Concomitantly, the imaginative vigor of his early writing has been shunted into a metaphoric style that is too often slapdash, sometimes even gibberish. Passages of graceless abstraction especially burden his more recent prose.

John Gardner was a self-conscious spokesman for the "life-affirming" novel in a period when affirmation is not the norm. *The Resurrection* (1966), his first published novel, established Gardner's great question: How does one affirm life with responsible intelligence in the face of life's denial? That question disturbs almost all of Gardner's major characters—Taggert Hodge in *The Sunlight Dialogues* (1972), Henry Soames in *Nickel Mountain* (1973), James Page in *October Light* (1976), Professor Peter Mickelsson in *Mickelsson's Ghosts* (1982). But Gardner made a poor case for the upbeat novel, inasmuch as he wearied his readers with leaden philosophizing and with Yankee rustics unable to carry the burden of his outsize stories. Ironically, he is at his best in short, *un*realistic tales, such as *Grendel* (1971) and "The King's Indian" (1974). The first is a fine retelling of the Beowulf story from the monster's bleakly poetic point of view; the second, a parody of classic sea-going

stories such as they might have been written by the metafic-
tionist writers Gardner considered decadent.

A veteran of the 1960s counterculture movements, Robert
Stone has written three novels that dwell in a general way on
the physical and psychological destructiveness of the American
imperium. *A Hall of Mirrors* (1967), *Dog Soldiers* (1975), and
A Flag for Sunrise (1981) focus specifically on the conjunction
of individuals and national corruption. Stone's characters are
a displaced lot who turn to alcohol and drugs in their efforts
to survive. The Vietnam involvement burns deep scars into
their psyches, and they find the web of American destructiveness everywhere—even in their own souls. Stone's vision of
America is much like Ken Kesey's, but his prose is more muscular, more grimly realistic, more unrelievedly serious, and his
bitterness is more naked. A marine-turned-drug-pusher lies
dying at the end of *Dog Soldiers*, his heroin stolen by a rene-
gade lawman, and he says, "They want you dead. . . . If you
can't get your own off them, then don't stand there and let them
spit on you, don't give them the satisfaction."

The traditions of naturalism and realism also influence
novels by James Dickey (b. 1923), John Rechy (b. 1934), Hubert
Selby, Jr. (b. 1928), and Paul Theroux (b. 1941). Dickey is essentially a poet, but his novel *Deliverance* (1970) is a masterful
narrative about four men besieged by mountaineers while exploring a North Georgia river. Rechy's *City of Night* (1963) is
a naturalist's survey of downtown Los Angeles, its thieves,
murderers, and transvestites; his *Rushes* (1979) is an even
darker survey of the sadomasochistic demimonde. Selby's *Last
Exit to Brooklyn* (1964) is a fine aggregate of stories about the
poor and the perverted, and Theroux's sardonic novels about
men and women caught up in alien cultures, most notably *The
Mosquito Coast* (1982), have an authority informed by the author's checkered career in the Peace Corps. Such works are
evidence that the naturalistic impulse still runs deep in American literature, and that naturalism can still command stylistic
grace.

NOVELISTS OF MANNERS

The novel of manners is a nice complement to naturalism and realism in the postwar period, for it is similarly devoted to illuminating the real world and similarly sensitive to the Neanderthal that lurks beneath the human skin. Its special attention to the behavioral codes of upper-class urban baili-wicks is not born in this period of social conservatism, as is sometimes thought, but of a pseudonaturalistic passion for ar-raigning the upper classes. The most distinguished practition-ers of the postwar novel of manners are James Gould Cozzens, whom I have already discussed as a naturalist manqué, John P. Marquand (1893–1960), Louis Auchincloss (b. 1917), John Cheever (1912–1982), J. D. Salinger (b. 1919), and John Updike (b. 1932). Joyce Carol Oates (b. 1938), Mary Gordon (b. 1949), John Kennedy Toole (1937–1969), and J. P. Donleavy (b. 1926) are novelists of manners interested in the less-moneyed classes.

John P. Marquand aspired to write a *comédie humaine*— "a series of novels," he said, "that would give a picture of a segment of America during the past fifty years." If he did not achieve such Balzacian sweep with his twenty-four novels, his postwar fictions *Point of No Return* (1949), *Melville Goodwin, U.S.A.* (1951), *Sincerely, Willis Wayde* (1955), *Women and Thomas Harrow* (1958), and *Timothy Dexter Revisited* (1960) depict the lives of the *haut bourgeois* who live in New York City and the environs of Boston, and each novel is carefully constructed of documentary facts that seemed to Marquand's contemporaries as enlightening as Balzac's sketches of the pro-vincial French. The past is an especially important element in Marquand's fiction, not because he was sentimentally attached to it, but because the disciplines esteemed in the past seemed to him a hedge against gathering chaos. Indeed, Marquand elected to write about the upper middle class not just because he knew it well, but because it seemed to him the last theater in which the conflict between social fixity and flux would be staged.

Louis Auchincloss has found his mentors in Henry James

and Edith Wharton, the novelists of old New York society. Labeling himself a Jacobite in deference to James's influence, Auchincloss writes urbane novels about the metropolitan rich caught up in situations where the law, finance, and family come into conflict. Novels such as *Portrait in Brownstone* (1962), *The Rector of Justin* (1964), *The Partners* (1974), and *Watchfires* (1982) evoke James's wit and intelligence in their setting of moral problems, subtlety and insight in characterization, and insider's knowledge of society. A Wall Street lawyer and a Social Registrant himself, Auchincloss seems especially fascinated by the freedom a more spacious world once allowed the moneyed *haut monde*. Half in love with those who dared to rule imperiously, he likes to tell their story in a dynastic sweep, often from the viewpoint of a younger and deluded hanger-on. Auchincloss himself never dares more than he can safely manage, but a finely crafted prose and an elegant dispassion compensate for the absence of fireworks in his novels. It is a patent absurdity that the world he depicts is thought irrelevant and that his critique of that world is thought softened by his affection for its monsters.

John Cheever tended to follow the middle-management employees barely noticed in Auchincloss's novels as they board their trains and head for homes in suburban New York and Connecticut. In the short stories collected in *The Housebreaker of Shady Hill* (1958) and *The Brigadier and the Golf Widow* (1964), Cheever liked to disturb his suburbanites with sudden eruptions of the grotesque. Ovid resolves their love lives; grotesquely allegorical figures drop in at their cocktail parties; and witches and wood nymphs live cozily down their streets. In the serial novels *The Wapshot Chronicle* (1957) and *The Wapshot Scandal* (1964), and in *Bullet Park* (1969), Cheever is virtually a puppeteer of the grotesque, incessantly manipulating ironies, comedies, and tragedies that lie tenebrously in wait for his characters.

Cheever's best work is *Falconer* (1977), a novel about the incarceration of Professor Ezekiel Farragut for the murder of his brother. Structured largely as a series of monologues by prisoners, guards, and assorted visitors to Falconer Prison, it is architecturally more impressive than Cheever's earlier work and psychologically more profound. Farragut's eventual release, not only from prison but from a serious drug habit, is so richly metaphoric a celebration of the human spirit that it makes Cheever's earlier fiction seem underworked.

Like Cheever, J. D. Salinger is attracted to the serial narrative. In several of his short stories, and in the longer tales that make up *Franny and Zooey* (1961) and *Raise High the Roof Beam, Carpenters; and Seymour: An Introduction* (1963), he develops a narrative about the Glass children, an extraordinary array of siblings whose suprasensibility catches them up in an ominous comedy of manners. Not only do their intellectual lives obsess the Glass children, but also their growth in aery, Buddhistic virtue. The stories pay a certain debt to cuteness, but that toll is easily forgiven for the sheer lovability of the characters. Their telltale gestures, their comedic inadequacies, their gamy, adolescent philosophizing—all receive elaborate, ungrudged attention.

On the strength of his first and only novel, *The Catcher in the Rye* (1951), Salinger acquired for 1950s collegians the kind of significance Fitzgerald and Hemingway had for collegians in the 1920s. *Catcher* is the story of sixteen-year-old Holden Caulfield, just expelled from prep school, who in the course of forty-eight hours in New York City comes to terms with a society he thinks decadent. Much of the novel's original appeal lay with the questions Holden asks, which seemed to 1950s youth peculiarly their own. Is it possible to live sincerely? To function with childhood integrity in the grown-up world? To drop out and let the world go by, uncontaminated by the films, the schools, the corrupting adults? The novel's appeal today rests somewhat more with its language. Salinger's ear for adolescent speech patterns is without equal, and though his characters are monuments to maladjustment, their cries for love and understanding transcend their amateur swearing and totemistic repetition. Crude, slangy, even imprecise, their lingua franca is as potent a language as the novel of manners affords.

Like Cheever and Salinger, John Updike first gained an audience in the pages of *The New Yorker*. More committed to rationality than either of his cohorts, Updike has more completely abandoned a *New Yorker* fondness for stories that merely nuance moments of feeling. Indeed, he typically encourages his readers to appreciate the continuing, everyday drama of his characters, and in a crisply probing idiom and with elaborate narrative scaffolding he directs our attention to characters we might otherwise overlook: the institutionalized aged of *The Poorhouse Fair* (1959); the bored adulterers of *Couples* (1968); the aging athlete "Rabbit" Angstrom in the trilogy *Rabbit Run* (1960), *Rabbit Redux* (1971), and *Rabbit Is Rich* (1981).

As Updike himself has pointed out, each of his novels is precisely dated and linked to a presidential administration with which it shares a spirit. *The Centaur* (1963) is indubitably a Truman novel; *Rabbit Run*, an Eisenhower; *Couples*, a Kennedy. Such relentless temporality runs deep in the life of Updike's fiction and seems somehow a failure of his imagination to transcend its immediate context, as if he had written too many "Talk of the Town" columns for *The New Yorker*. *Bech: A Book* (1970) agonizes in the fashion of its year over the writer's profession; *Museums and Women* (1972) imitates in the fashion of its year the narrative experiments of John Barth; and *Marry Me* (1976) employs three different endings in the fashionable open-endedness of its year. Updike has long been concerned with the relationship between religious belief and the secularism of modern life, but even secularism troubles him less in his recent work than it had before, the quotidian *fact* of secularism apparently limiting his imagination now, like too many other facts and fashions.

Still, Updike is a writer of prodigious competence. His uncluttered paragraphs and pages advance with seductive rhythm and exact pitch to their last commonplace perception. Wonderfully luminous images and metaphors irradiate this advance and make even Rabbit's basketball games seem significant and beautiful. In an era of moral confusion, he has succeeded as a moralist without radically debunking our mores, and in an age of rampant theory, he is an intellectual who has successfully disdained abstraction.

Joyce Carol Oates's fiction is not easily classified. The importance of social and economic facts in novels such as *With Shuddering Fall* (1964), *Expensive People* (1968), and *them* (1969) suggests that she is a social realist, but a series of novels about the great professions—*Wonderland* (1971), *Do with Me What You Will* (1973), and *The Assassins* (1975)—suggests as forcefully that she is a novelist of manners. A gothic predilection for madness and violence complicates her literary allegiances, as does a battle between feminine passivity and male domination that she stages relentlessly. Oates's work is in fact a preeminent example of the tendency of naturalism and realism to confound literary categories by finding contemporary expression in the novel of manners.

It is very nearly as difficult to assess Oates's achievement as to classify it. Her vision of people unable to articulate their sense of oppression is compelling, almost worthy of Dreiser, and she has a resourceful imagination, apparently capable of embodying this vision in an endless outpouring of stories about life's cruel changeability. But Oates's narrative sophistication waxes and wanes. Capable of clarity and grace, she is equally capable of hysterically incoherent sentimentalism. Capable of dense psychological detail, she is equally capable of sensationalistic balderdash. One suspects her of impatience. Rushing headlong into print with novels, short stories, poetry, critical essays, and book reviews, she apparently takes too little time to understand, to shape, and to revise.

Mary Gordon has only recently appeared on the literary scene, but in two novels about women and the Roman Catholic church she has established herself as a feminist J. F. Powers. *Final Payments* (1978) is about Isabel Moore's emergence into the world after caring for her deeply religious father for eleven years. *The Company of Women* (1981) is about six women drawn together by a complexly eccentric priest and about one of their number, the youngest, who makes a bid to be free.

Without involving herself in radical polemic, Gordon limns beautifully the need of her women to escape from men in all of their roles—father, husband, lover, priest, God. Technical weaknesses cause her novels to sag in the middle, but imagination and intelligence are layered so thickly in her prose that we are hardly aware of architectural lapses.

John Kennedy Toole took his life before a publisher was found for his first and only novel, *A Confederacy of Dunces* (1980), and this comic masterpiece would have been lost had not his mother pressed it on the novelist Walker Percy, who recognized its quality and aided in its publication. It is the story of a self-defined genius, Ignatius J. Reilly, who wants to reform the mores of the twentieth century but has to acquire a job when his mother insists that at the age of thirty he earn his keep. That bourgeois goal becomes an epic task in virtue of Reilly's blithering contempt for Freud, for Protestants, for Hollywood and the United States government, for homosexuals *and* heterosexuals—his contempt, in short, for the postmedieval world. With his gifted sense of the mock heroic, Toole renders his cantankerous Don Quixote a winning creation.

Toole would appear to owe a small debt to J. P. Donleavy, a novelist who renounced his American citizenship in 1967 in favor of his parents' native Ireland. *The Ginger Man* (1955) established Donleavy as a master of the comic picaresque. Sebastian Dangerfield, his protagonist, is a roguish egomaniac who will not compromise his spirit to gain the material success he wants. Greedy, lustful, dishonest, he represents man courageously faithful to himself whatever his amorality and whatever society's judgments. He is the prototype of characters in *A Singular Man* (1963), *The Beastly Beatitudes of Balthazar B.* (1968), *A Fairy Tale of New York* (1973), and *The Destinies of Darcy Dancer, Gentleman* (1977). Indeed, he is too much their prototype. Despite stylistic vigor, the novels Donleavy has published in the wake of *The Ginger Man* have a staleness about them as disconcerting as their whiff of mortality.

The novel of manners enjoys a vigorous postwar life not only in the works discussed above, but also in popular novels like Laura Z. Hobson's (b. 1900) *Gentleman's Agreement* (1947), Sloan Wilson's (b. 1920) *The Man in the Gray Flannel Suit* (1955), and Alison Lurie's (b. 1926) *The War between the Tates* (1974). It survives with special vigor in detective fiction, notably in the novels of Ross Macdonald (Kenneth Millar, b. 1915) and Joseph Hansen (b. 1923). Far from being dead, as is often claimed, the novel of manners remains an important voice in defining the changing and varied forms of American life.

If naturalism, realism, and the novel of manners are the enduring mountains in American fiction, ethnicity is the epicenter. Indeed, since the mid-1940s, American novelistic literatures have been ethnically based in such a way as to recall the groundswell of regionalism in the last century. Such literatures tend to flout the values of the mainstream culture, which partially explains their mystique. Progress, egalitarianism, and logic are esteemed less in ethnic fictions than are tradition and ceremony. Romantic love and conventional morality are valued less than a sense of person and community. The cadences of regional speech, especially in the folkways of gossip and declamation, are their particular treasure, and a sense of oral story is often their narrative strength. Southern, Jewish, and black schools of ethnic fiction have been especially important in recent decades.

SOUTHERN FICTION

William Faulkner (1897–1962) is the *éminence grise* of postwar Southern fiction, even though his best work was written between the two world wars. *Intruder in the Dust* (1948), *Knight's Gambit* (1949), *Requiem for a Nun* (1951), *The Town* (1957), *The Mansion* (1959), and *The Reivers* (1962) constitute a cycle of novels set in a make-believe county in north Mississippi called Yoknapatawpha, but as a group these novels do not equal those in an earlier Yoknapatawpha cycle, which includes *The Sound and the Fury* (1929), *Light in August* (1932), and

Go Down, Moses (1942). It is not altogether clear why Faulkner's writing declined after the publication of *Go Down, Moses*, but it would be a mistake to link its decline to World War II, for the general impact of the war on Faulkner and on Southern literature was not profound. Still, it is a simple fact that the work of Faulkner and every other Southern writer who was prominent between the world wars diminished in quality after the mid-1940s. One might cite illustratively the writings of Katherine Anne Porter (1890–1980), whose novel *Ship of Fools* (1962) lacks the mandarin control of her earlier short fiction, and Robert Penn Warren (b. 1905), whose more recent fiction is vastly inferior to *All the King's Men* (1946).

Faulkner's status as an *éminence grise* has been something of a difficulty for Southern writers younger than he, just as Joyce's towering achievement posed a difficulty for younger modernists who continued to work Joyce's idiom. "Nobody wants his mule and wagon stalled on the same track the Dixie Limited is roaring down," Flannery O'Connor remarked in a homey allusion to Faulkner's oeuvre. But what other route was left to younger Southern novelists? Faulkner's peopling of Yoknapatawpha with characters caught up in a myth of vanished glory was so definitive in the literary mind that striking any radically different note about Southern consciousness seemed wrongheaded. Southern literature in the postwar years has therefore a homogenous quality born not only of a traditionalist society but of circumscribed possibilities.

Three women novelists not only held their own in the hard light of Faulkner's eminence but built major reputations: Eudora Welty (b. 1909), Flannery O'Connor (1925–1964), and Carson McCullers (1917–1967). They survived on the same track as the Dixie Limited not simply because they were greatly talented, but because they explored more delicate nuances of feeling than Faulkner and avoided his heroic scale.

Eudora Welty's stories tend to portray individuals, families, and even whole communities that resist the pressures of historical change. In novels such as *Delta Wedding* (1946) and in story collections such as *The Bride of Innisfallen* (1955), she employs a social perception as finely tuned as her varied and subtle technique. Her characters are doomed by the clock, but memory enables them to hold the clock at bay, and memory is for them a mode of survival. Eccentric, intensely self-aware, doomed to watch the South collapse around them, they are capable of comic high spirits, as in *The Ponder Heart* (1954), and of ultimate reconciliation, as in the sparely beautiful novel *The Optimist's Daughter* (1972). Monologic short stories such as "Why I Live at the P.O." (1941) are uproarious tributes to Welty's command of the vernacular. Welty's fiction is disarmingly modest, for it tends to discount moral judgment and to be written on a small scale. Her technical inventiveness, however, is enormous. Her expert discussions of craft, as in *The Eye of the Story* (1978), are evidence of her narrative sophistication, and though laudation has never been to her taste, she is incontestably the reigning grande dame of Southern letters.

Flannery O'Connor was a deeply religious Roman Catholic, but her ill-favored characters experience an eruption of God into their lives with a violence more typical of Bible-Belt Protestantism than of her natal faith. O'Connor's Georgians even tend to exult in their malfeasance and unregenerate willfulness. Cantankerousness is as fundamental a mode of being for them as myth is for Faulkner's characters and memory for Welty's. "The Life You Save May Be Your Own" (1953), "Good Country People" (1955), "The Artificial Nigger" (1955): to name the stories collected in *A Good Man Is Hard to Find* (1955), *Everything That Rises Must Converge* (1965), and finally in *The Complete Stories* (1971) is to list the most anthologized short fiction of their period. Her novels *Wise Blood* (1952) and *The Violent Bear It Away* (1960) are less successful. Although mordant in their interplay between disbelief and the saving ways of grace, they seem thinly textured in comparison with the effervescently acerbic short stories, for the scale of the stories renders the bite of O'Connor's humor more successfully and renders her whimsically unsentimental tone more startling. The protagonists of the stories tend to experience revelations about themselves rather than the revelation of God experienced in the novels, but it is never clear that revelations about the self are not also revelations of God, and O'Connor's tales are always amenable to such theological interpretation. Her best fiction depends upon a mixed effect—an incongruity between style and subject that she achieves by turning a poker face to the extraordinary.

Carson McCullers was more truly the untutored provincial that Flannery O'Connor pretended to be, but like her Georgian colleague she was interested in the dark corners of the mind and employed the grotesque as a heartfelt metaphor for loneliness. Her best stories, *The Heart Is a Lonely Hunter* (1940), "The Ballad of the Sad Café" (1943), and *The Member of the Wedding* (1946), are striking in their evocation of hermetically sealed lives and in their disbelief in love's ability to redeem lives irrevocably turned inward. But *Reflections in a Golden Eye* (1941) and *Clock without Hands* (1961) suffer *ad extremis* the weaknesses of McCullers's art: her pretentious philosophizing, her deficient sense of prose rhythm, her hypertrophied artifice. Because formerly inflated, McCullers's reputation is now in decline, but no one has written more feelingly than she about the lot of the eccentric, and no one has written with more compassion about adolescent loneliness and desperation.

Roman Catholic writers have been notably influential in contemporary Southern literature, perhaps because their religious sensibility reverences the sense of tradition dear to the Southern mind. Flannery O'Connor is the most celebrated of them, but Walker Percy (b. 1916), Caroline Gordon (1895–1981), and John William Corrington (b. 1932) have also written fiction informed by a Catholic perspective.

Walker Percy dislikes being classified as a Southern novelist, for he is deeply influenced by philosophical existentialism and owes a greater debt to French and Russian novelists than to Faulkner. He entirely avoids Faulknerian stylistics, in fact, and seldom invokes local color. Yet Percy's characters are unmistakably Southern—borderline grotesques who work out their salvation as carefully as Flannery O'Connor's eccentrics. Moreover, Percy's stories can be read, like O'Connor's, as religious and philosophical advocacy.

Percy has published five novels: *The Moviegoer* (1961), *The Last Gentleman* (1966), *Love in the Ruins* (1971), *Lancelot* (1977), and *The Second Coming* (1980). All are graceful, understated works, but the first of them is still Percy's masterpiece. Its moviegoing hero fights to maintain his personal sense of human existence amid real-world clichés of ambition, devoutness, and etiquette that threaten to swamp his consciousness. In motion pictures he discovers a shadow world, preferable to reality because it is "cleaner," more innocent than life of extraneous ideology. Films are for Percy's hero what memory is for Welty's characters, but the two authors' attitudes toward the South are very different. The badge of defeatedness, old-fashionedness, and underdevelopment worn so proudly by the South in Welty's fiction recurs in Percy's novels as a badge of alienation from the South itself—in its latter-day phase a land of bankers and corporation executives. The modern South seems to Percy as amoral and as ahistorical as any other section of the country.

Caroline Gordon was not prolific after 1945, and her late fiction has generally been regarded as insignificant. But *The Strange Children* (1951), *The Malefactors* (1956), and *The Glory of Hera* (1972) are an interesting footnote to the Agrarian movement that was launched in the 1920s by a group that included Allen Tate, Gordon's onetime husband. Specifically, Gordon's postwar novels suggest a modified allegiance to the conservative Agrarian ideal and a de facto acceptance of the modern South, not unlike Percy's acceptance. Gordon was always concerned with ideal orders, but religion and myth came to replace Agrarian economics as ordering elements in her imagination.

Although somewhat better known as a poet, John William Corrington writes novels and short fiction of a metaphysical and theological cast as well. His best novel is *The Upper Hand*

(1967), the story of a priest who quits the church and descends into a metaphorical hell of dope peddlers, prostitutes, and abortionists. Corrington's other novels—*And Wait for the Night* (1964) and *The Bombardier* (1970)—treat respectively of the last days of the Civil War and the bombing of Dresden in World War II. Their compounding of Corrington's religious and historical sensibilities produces an array of dark paradoxes and grotesqueries, and some very funny scenes. Corrington's short stories, collected in *The Lonesome Traveler* (1968) and *The Actes and Monuments* (1978), are also impressive.

The acceptance of the modern South in the fiction of Walker Percy and Caroline Gordon seems a final obsequy for the Southern Renaissance, a flowering of letters that was inspired by a myth of the Old South and that survived in full blossom, always looking backward, from the 1920s until World War II. In a kindred acceptance, a number of Southern writers who began as regionalists have turned to interests not identifiably Southern in their more recent work. William Styron (b. 1925), Elizabeth Spencer (b. 1921), Truman Capote (b. 1924), Shirley Ann Grau (b. 1929), and Calder Willingham (b. 1922) can be numbered among them.

William Styron has demonstrated considerable boldness in working with materials not endemic to the Southern writer. Although his early works, notably *Lie Down in Darkness* (1951), were influenced by Faulkner in their unexpected shafts of poetry, Styron's most recent novels have seized new ground intransigently. *The Confessions of Nat Turner* (1967) is a fictional account of the 1831 slave rebellion led by the real-life slave Nat Turner, and it thereby appropriates materials black novelists tend to claim as their exclusive province. *Sophie's Choice* (1979) is narrated by a would-be writer from Virginia, but its subject partakes of the Holocaust legacy Jewish writers regard as their domain: the title character is a Polish Catholic woman who survives Auschwitz and later becomes involved with an American Jewish man obsessed with the Holocaust. Styron's novels have been the subject of some acrimonious debate because of this ethnic trespassing, but their factual accuracy, their careful plotting, and their linguistic polish merit critical respect.

Elizabeth Spencer began her career with three novels set in Mississippi: *Fire in the Morning* (1948), *The Crooked Way* (1952), and *The Voice at the Back Door* (1957). Intricately woven and substantial narratives, they are largely in the tradition of the Southern Renaissance and show the influence of Faulkner and Welty. With *The Light in the Piazza* (1960) and *Knights and Dragons* (1965), Spencer turned to international settings and a Jamesian formula of innocent Americans set loose in Europe. *No Place for an Angel* (1967) continues her interest in displaced Americans, as does *The Snare* (1972), which is set in New Orleans, perhaps the only European city in America. Because she likes to experiment, Spencer's novels have been more varied in both theme and technique than this increasing concern with possibilities of life beyond the American ken might lead one to expect.

Like Styron and Spencer, Truman Capote began his career writing distinctively Southern tales. The novels *Other Voices, Other Rooms* (1948) and *The Grass Harp* (1951) and the story collection *A Tree of Night* (1949) contain delicately gothic stories about isolated sensibilities—stories located somewhere between decadence and sentimentality. Capote broke this Southern mold with *Breakfast at Tiffany's* (1958), a charming bonbon about an unprofessional prostitute named Holly Golightly. *In Cold Blood* (1966) completed his break with Southern material. The elaborately researched account of a multiple murder that occurred in Kansas in 1959, it is a work of curious sympathies but great power. Capote christened it a "nonfiction novel" and in a fit of self-promotion claimed he had invented a new literary form. *In Cold Blood* has not that distinction, but it is still one of the darkest and most compelling documentaries in American literature, and its compounding of factuality and art has been widely imitated.

Shirley Ann Grau has been less successful than Capote in breaking with the Southern school of fiction, but her break is also more tentative than his. To date she has published five novels: *The Hard Blue Sky* (1958), *The House on Coliseum Street* (1961), *The Keepers of the House* (1964), *The Condor Passes* (1971), and *Evidence of Love* (1977). All but the last are Southern in locale and atmosphere, as are the majority of Grau's short stories, collected in *The Black Prince* (1955) and *The Wind Shifting West* (1973). The Southern ambience seems crucial to Grau's success, inasmuch as her warm feeling for the land and its folkways counteracts the chill of her attenuated stylistics, undramatic plots, and elaborately precise descriptions of nature. *Evidence of Love*, her first major work to be set outside the South, is the least successful of her novels.

Calder Willingham is the only one of this group of writers who does not seem to find his Southern niche confining. His first novel, *End as a Man* (1947), is a fine, satiric portrait of a Southern military academy, and *To Eat a Peach* (1955) and *Rambling Rose* (1972) are also Southern novels, amiably comic and comfortably unpretentious. Willingham's masterpiece is probably *Eternal Fire* (1963). A gorgeously overripe exercise in Southern Gothicism, it is crammed with sex, incest, miscegenation, murder, and suicide and constitutes a frolicsome parody of its genre. Willingham works in a less Southern mode with apparently equal ease. *Natural Child* (1952) is a New York novel of some distinction, and *Geraldine Bradshaw* (1950), *Reach to the Stars* (1951), and *The Big Nickel* (1975) are a popular comedic series about Dick Davenport, California bellhop extraordinaire in the first two novels, published author in the third.

Although the foregoing novelists turn self-consciously to non-Southern material, a large number of writers remain committed to exploring the Southern consciousness, its indomitable will to remember, its metaphysics of survival. The occasional magnolia blossom is an inescapable component of their art, but so is a realism that knows sentimentalism for what it is. Peter Taylor (b. 1917?), Cormac McCarthy (b. 1933), and Reynolds Price (b. 1933) are prominent among such writers. Less prominent, because less entirely committed to fiction, are

Andrew Lytle (b. 1902), Marion Montgomery (b. 1925), Shelby Foote (b. 1916), and David Madden (b. 1933).

Peter Taylor's *Collected Stories* (1969) is an admirable selection of the short fiction he published in a series of prior collections—*A Long Fourth* (1948), for instance, and *Miss Lenora When Last Seen* (1963). Taylor's usual subject is the end of the genteel order, and his characters are citizens of Nashville or Memphis, usually deeply civilized losers. Without sentimentalizing Old South notions of loyalty and dignity, and without resorting to grotesquerie, Taylor makes it clear that change and its attendant accommodations cost the human spirit no less dearly than living in the past. His stories include too many clichés about old family retainers and indomitable matriarchs, but Taylor's unsentimental sympathy for his losers gives his fiction a nice crispness, pleasantly free of rhetoric.

Cormac McCarthy has established himself as an important Southern writer on the basis of his four novels: *The Orchard Keeper* (1965), *Outer Dark* (1968), *Child of God* (1974), and *Suttree* (1979). All are in the tradition of gothic pastoral, intense in characterization, extravagant in plotting, profoundly attentive to a mystique of the land. *Child of God* is especially gothic, for its main character is a necrophile who kills people in order to possess them sexually. The title character in *Suttree* echoes him quietly. His twin brother having died at birth, Suttree is convinced (and not without reason) that death is his shadow self. McCarthy's particular talent is to make such characters representative of ordinary human needs. If profoundly misbegotten, they are not for that reason less involved in the human situation.

Reynolds Price is often compared to Faulkner, primarily because of his fondness for the dynastic narrative, but also on the bases of his feeling for the rural South and his biblical and mythic paradigms. His first two novels, *A Long and Happy Life* (1962) and *A Generous Man* (1966), chronicle the Mustian family; his more recent novels, *The Surface of Earth* (1975) and *The Source of Light* (1981), chronicle the Kendal and Mayfield families, culminating in the latter novel with the fourth-generation story of Hutchins Mayfield, a youthful North Carolina poet. Price's incessant theme is the capacity of the self to survive the ironies and contradictions of life. Somber, romantic, but loving too much the convolutions of narratives within narratives, he is an important novelist but one whose multiplicity of purpose sometimes outstrips his control.

A classmate of Robert Penn Warren and a student of John Crowe Ransom, Andrew Lytle was briefly involved in 1921 with the Vanderbilt University Fugitives, a group of young men who were trying to develop a school of Southern poetry, and he is to this day an Agrarian of fiercely conservative views. Not exclusively a novelist, he has written critical essays, a biography of Bedford Forrest, and a magisterial chronicle of his family entitled *A Wake for the Living* (1975). His oeuvre is dominated by the two postwar novels, *A Name for Evil* (1947) and *The Velvet Horn* (1957). Both are elaborately plotted, almost Jamesian artifacts. A popular confusion of Lytle's conservative views with his fictional statements has branded the novels culturally retrograde, but the actual rhetoric of his novels is based less on Agrarian economic views than on the Garden of Eden myth.

Marion Montgomery is almost unknown outside the South, but his works of fiction bespeak a commitment to Southern ideology deeply respected by novelists such as Flannery O'Connor, Erskine Caldwell, and Walker Percy. His poetry and criticism are no less passionately regional than his novels and enjoy a similar respect on their home ground. Montgomery's Southern commitment takes a serious narrative toll, however, and the novels *The Wandering of Desire* (1962), *Ye Olde Bluebird* (1967), and *Fugitive* (1974) are riddled with digressions, anecdotes, and philosophizing about the South almost impossible for anyone not a Southern ideologue to accept as narratively valid.

A classmate and longtime friend of Walker Percy, Shelby Foote published a series of four novels and a story sequence before turning to the composition of his three-volume history, *The Civil War: A Narrative* (1958, 1963, 1974). *Tournament*

(1949), *Follow Me Down* (1950), *Love in a Dry Season* (1951), *Shiloh* (1952), and the sequence *Jordan County* (1954) are all studies of the changing South, variously emphasizing its shift from a farming society to a business community, from chivalric values to moneyed values, and from fundamentalist morality to modern sexual freedom. All the novels are emphatically realistic, and all but *Shiloh* are set in the eponymous Jordan County, Mississippi. Foote's most recent novel is *September September* (1978), a story of interracial kidnapping set against the backdrop of Little Rock, Arkansas, in the fateful September of 1957 when federal troops descended on the city to enforce racial integration of the schools. Like the young Faulkner before him, Foote is more esteemed in France than in the United States, especially for his early novel *Follow Me Down*, which is a complex series of monologues inspired by Browning's *The Ring and the Book* and generally thought to be his best work.

David Madden's creative energy seems boundless, for he is the prolific author of novels, short stories, poetry, drama, literary criticism, and film scripts. Individually, Madden's fictions suffer from this plentitude, for they are typically worked in several versions, sometimes even in various media, and their narrative coherence is tentative and irresolute, as if to accommodate this nomadic ranging. *Cassandra Singing* (1969) has existed in at least seventeen versions, as both drama and fiction. *Brothers in Confidence* (1972) is an expanded version of the novella "Traven" (1968) and was later incorporated whole into the novel *Pleasure-Dome* (1979), which is a sequel to the autobiographical novel *Bijou* (1974). *Pleasure-Dome* was begun as an attempt to combine six works of fiction, some published, some unwritten, but ended as a combination of *Brothers in Confidence* and the novella "Nothing Dies but Something Mourns" (1968). *On the Big Wind* (1980) is an assemblage of seven comic episodes, most of them previously published. If individually these works are less than marmoreal, together they make up an impressive meditation on the relationship between imagination and life. That Madden subjects his fiction to ever-new imaginings is not inappropriate to his underlying, eminently Southern theme—that the vital powers of human beings are weakened when they abjure their past.

The vigor of Southern fiction in the work of writers like Madden, Taylor, and Price does not mean that the Southern Renaissance survived the end of World War II. But the best writing in the South today continues to explore the main themes of the Renaissance: the past as legend, and the sense of lost tradition. This steady focus speaks eloquently of the culture's will to survive, if only in its best parts, and if only in memory.

JEWISH FICTION

Urban, northern, and liberal in its orientation, the contemporary Jewish novel balances the agrarian and conservative bias of the Southern novel. Not at ease with either traditional Jewish or modern American life, it tends to position itself between a commitment on one hand to the American mainstream and an unexpired commitment on the other hand to the East European *shtetl*. The Nazi holocaust and a religious destiny grown increasingly unreal are ghostly sources of its mood, and a sense of nonacculturation is its distinctive note. Saul Bellow (b. 1915), Bernard Malamud (b. 1914), and Philip Roth (b. 1933) dominate the Jewish novel, so much so that Bellow once referred to them as the Hart, Schaffner & Marx of American letters. With a Nobel Prize to cap his Pulitzer and three National Book Awards, Bellow is not only preeminent among them, but the most honored of living American novelists.

Bellow's first novel, *Dangling Man* (1944), purports to be the journal of a Chicagoan named Joseph who "dangles" between civilian and military status during World War II because his enlistment is snarled in red tape. Joseph also dangles between intelligence and will, between knowledge and experience, and between docility and rebellion. He is the quintessential Bellow character—a man torn by divergent impulses and so deeply introspective that his dealings with the world tend to be irrationally passionate. The heroes of *The Victim* (1947), *Henderson the Rain King* (1959), *Herzog* (1964), and *The Dean's December* (1982) struggle through similar dialectics, and they do so without resolution, for Bellow seems to regard nonacculturation as an inescapable condition of human existence. Perhaps further to convey this sense of life's dividedness, Bellow tends to publish sunlit, optimistic novels in alternation with darker works—*The Adventures of Augie March* (1953) and *Humboldt's Gift* (1975), for instance, in alternation with *Seize the Day* (1956) and *Mr. Sammler's Planet* (1970).

Humboldt's Gift, a fictional portrait of the late poet Delmore Schwartz, is in many ways typical of Bellow's novels, arguably his finest work. It has the vitality of *Augie March* and the weariness with the intractable claims of life in *Mr. Sammler's Planet*, the comic hyperbole of *Henderson* and the autobiographical resonance of *The Dean's December*. As in all of Bellow's novels, the language of *Humboldt's Gift* is a compound of street slang and learned abstractions that admirably suits Bellow's chiaroscuric swings of mood. Partly because of this chiaroscuro, but also because of a typically outsize hero and a passion for problems of the spirit, *Humboldt's Gift* can withstand a comparison with Dostoevsky's novels that seems de rigueur in criticism of Bellow's novels.

In Bernard Malamud's fiction, Bellow's Dangling Man becomes The Outsider—the rube in the big city, the alien in the ethnic neighborhood, the not-really-religious Jew. This character may transport himself to Kiev, Rome, Brooklyn, or Vermont, but he carries the psychological scar of his outsider's status with him, and like the Dangling Man he learns to live in the battle zone between hope and calamity. Because Malamud has a Jewish sensitivity to the language of poignancy and loss, his rendering of such characters' lives is masterful. No one catches as well as he those moments when the heart must recognize its hopes as vain.

Malamud is no celebrant of the schlemiel, however much his characters may superficially resemble that stock character of Jewish humor. His characters are involved in more serious battle than is the schlemiel, and Malamud is grimly moralistic about their fates. In *The Assistant* (1957), *A New Life* (1961), *The Fixer* (1966), and *Dubin's Lives* (1979), he devises object lessons in the acceptance of moral responsibility; in *The Natural* (1952) and *The Tenants* (1971) he devises parables of moral failure. *The Fixer* is his most eloquent novel. Based on the 1913 trial of a Kiev Jew for the murder of a Christian child, it pits the pathetic "fixer" Yakov Bok (his surname means "goat") against the entire enormity of human injustice in order to distill Bok's spiritual salvation. Malamud is at his best in working with such lore. The archetypal framework restrains his moral indignation and seems to release the full richness of his style, both the Yiddish cadences that subtly shape its rhythms and the language of ancient morality that lends weight to its diction. Malamud has not the range of Bellow, either stylistically or intellectually, but his moral vision in such works as *The Fixer* probes a depth of Jewish experience that Bellow does not attempt.

Philip Roth belongs to a generation of writers younger than Bellow and Malamud, in spirit as well as in years. Less concerned than they with the mystique of being Jewish and more concerned with the emotional dynamics of a Jewish rearing, he gives voice to the Jewish libido as it wages a losing battle with guilt, sexual confusion, and thralldom to the family. The critical success of the collection *Goodbye, Columbus* (1959) and the novel *Letting Go* (1962) launched Roth's career, but it was *Portnoy's Complaint* (1969) that established him as a spokesman for aggrieved Jewish sons. A blend of hyperbole, ribald humor, and textbook Freudianism, it transforms Alexander Portnoy's "complaint" into anti-Semitic farce. Portnoy's problem is essentially his Jewish mother. His impatience with her fades abruptly into outrage, his outrage into paranoia, his paranoia into guilt, and it is Roth's genius to turn Portnoy's guilt into psychological slapstick. A desperate buffoonery is Portnoy's response to female terrorism, apparently Roth's as well.

My Life as a Man (1974) is Roth's most accomplished novel.

Its stratagem is that stories about a character named Nathan Zuckerman preface a story about their author—one Peter Tarnapol. In a Borgesian twist, Tarnapol's writings struggle vainly to illumine for their author what is wrong with his life, and few of Roth's fictions strike as successful a balance between comic lightness and morose gloom. *The Breast* (1972) succeeds in quite another mode. A Kafkaesque parable, it describes David Kepesh's metamorphosis into a gigantic mammary gland and amounts to a lesson in self-acceptance. Like all of Roth's more successful fictions, it is satirically attentive to exaggerated instances of American-Jewish culture and seismographically alert to the libidinal tic.

Less concerned than Bellow, Malamud, and Roth with the problems of Jewish-American acculturation, two important Jewish novelists strike independent paths. On one hand, E. L. Doctorow (b. 1931) is more interested in Americana than in Judaica; and on the other hand, the naturalized American Isaac Bashevis Singer (b. 1904) restricts himself almost entirely to writing about the *shtetl* life of European Jewry before the war.

Doctorow has carved a niche for himself in the temple of American nostalgia. After a bleakly poetic novel called *Welcome to Hard Times* (1960) and a misadventure in science fiction entitled *Big as Life* (1966), he came to critical attention with *The Book of Daniel* (1971), a fictionalized account of the convicted spies Julius and Ethel Rosenberg as it might have been written by one of their sons. In *Ragtime* (1975), Doctorow hit upon a formula more hospitable to the historical detail and the strong scenes that are his talent. A loosely woven story of three families during the Ragtime era, one WASP, one Jewish, and one black, it is a series of disjointed scenes with cameo appearances by such figures as Emma Goldman, Harry Houdini, and J. P. Morgan. While its fragmentary method eventually palls, *Ragtime* is a marvelous anthology of Americana, circa 1900, and an entertaining novelty.

Doctorow's *Loon Lake* (1980) is also a loosely structured novel, crammed in its turn with trappings of the 1930s. Its hero is a young man named Joe Korzeniowski (a curious nod to Joseph Conrad) who runs away from home, travels the rails, becomes entangled in union politics, and in general lives out the lore of 1930s naturalism. Unlike *Ragtime*, however, *Loon Lake* is a totally realized entity, sustained by a lyricism beautifully suited to its nostalgic mode. Its publication has elevated Doctorow to the rank of major novelist.

With some justification, the novels of Isaac Bashevis Singer tend to be understood as a continuing history of East European Jewry. *Satan in Goray* (translated 1943) and *The Slave* (translated 1962) reach back to the Chmielnicki pogroms in the seventeenth century; *The Family Moskat* (translated 1950) and *Shosha* (translated 1978) transpire in the last days before the Nazi takeover in Poland; *Enemies: A Love Story* (translated 1972) depicts the New York lives of Jews who escaped the Holocaust.

Singer is less a historical novelist than a conservator of the East European imagination—a conservator, too, of literary Yiddish, for all his novels are written in that language as if in epitaph for a nearly extinct readership. He is not specifically a conservator of the Hassidic imagination, as one might expect on the basis of his family background, but of an imagination older than the Hassidic tradition and not wholly distinct from pagan animism. Singer's short stories are more striking in this respect than his novels. Tense, melodramatic, sometimes gnomic, they deal in warlocks, demons, and dybbukim, witness to cabalism, demonic possession, and mysterious feats of telepathy. Without invoking Freud, the stories hint darkly that such atavistic imaginings are the shadow world of sexual repression. It is perhaps an illusion of his art, but Singer convinces one he is in touch with the primordial imagination. To read him is to sense the ancient link between story and magic.

Comic fiction has been a notable strength of Jewish writers since the war and has taken on what Matthew Arnold called "the tone of the center." The novels of Philip Roth might serve as a model of this fiction, with their tone of desperate joking, their mania, and their antic ferocity. Such comedy finds an

immediate antecedent in the borscht-circuit vaudevillians, but
it is linked with more imaginative largesse to the Jewish experience of oppression. Bruce Jay Friedman (b. 1930), Wallace
Markfield (b. 1926), Stanley Elkin (b. 1930), and Joseph Heller
(b. 1923) are prominent writers in the mode.

Bruce Jay Friedman's name is irrevocably linked to black
humor, both on the evidence of his novels and because he coined
the phrase in editing a 1965 miscellany of new fiction. *Black
humor* is a catchall term, but Friedman's own description of it
as a "one-foot in the asylum kind of fiction" catches nicely its
comic angst and its half-desperate delight in the illogical complications of life. In the novels *Stern* (1962), *A Mother's Kisses*
(1964), *The Dick* (1970), and the sequence *About Harry Towns*
(1974), Friedman invents characters blackly humorous in this
sense. Facing a world of suffering and misery, a world in which
anti-Semitism and racial prejudice entangle good intentions,
his protagonists cast themselves as movie heroes and respond
to the real world as if it were cinema vérité. Grand but pointless
gestures are their comic signature.

Wallace Markfield is as much an intellectual New York
prankster as Friedman is a black humorist. The parodic instinct runs deep in him, as well as a taste for one-liners, a taste
for Jewish expressions of perturbation, and a distaste for high-
brow cant. These elements come together brilliantly in *To an
Early Grave* (1964). A parody of the Hades chapter in *Ulysses*,
this comic novel tells of the journey of four Jewish intellectuals
into the depths of Brooklyn to attend the funeral of a friend,
of their madcap attendance at the wrong funeral, and of their
desecration of the friend's obsequies with a preposterous game
of one-upmanship. *Teitlebaum's Window* (1970) and *You Could
Live If They Let You* (1974) are somewhat less successful fictions in the same style, the first a Bildungsroman indebted to
Joyce's *A Portrait of the Artist as a Young Man*, the second a
goy's view of a vulgar Jewish comedian—Lenny Bruce in all
but name. *Multiple Orgasms* (1977), an unfinished novel about
a young woman's attempt to return a sweater to a department

store, suggests that Markfield would like to break with his specifically Jewish material.

"It is in the long sad tradition of my people to pluck laughter from despair," says one of Stanley Elkin's Jewish characters, and more than either Friedman or Markfield, Elkin draws upon a black humor traditional in Jewish comedy long before Friedman coined the term. In the novels *Boswell: A Modern Comedy* (1964), *A Bad Man* (1967), *The Dick Gibson Show* (1971), and *The Franchiser* (1976) his protagonists are picaros who collide with powers greater than they, with sickness, ultimately with death. Salesmen and promoters as a rule, his characters' *shtick* is the sales pitch, and they hurl it bravely into the face of absurdity, salesmanship virtually their metaphysic of life. Exactly pitched and richly metaphoric, the language of the salesman is one of the comic delights of Elkin's fiction.

Only superficially a war novel, Joseph Heller's *Catch-22* (1961) is less concerned with World War II than with the struggles of its hero, bombardier John Yossarian, to survive his ever-expanding tour of duty in the Army Air Corps. A blitz of forms, papers, regulations, and the alogical "catch-22" impede Yossarian's escape and represent institutionalized madness run amok. Bitter, hilarious, subversive, *Catch-22* is a sprawling and boisterously exaggerated novel and probably the most celebrated text in the black humor mode. Heller's subsequent novels, *Something Happened* (1974) and *Good as Gold* (1979), are less esteemed than *Catch-22* because they are less original in conception and technique. *Something Happened*, however, is a better novel than is generally thought. In this story of a life subtly gone awry, a life in which "something happened," the narrator's perplexity strikes deep into the heart.

Although many writers express dismay that their Jewishness should constitute a literary identity, the sheer number of Jews active in the ranks of American fiction remains demographically impressive. Writers who have gained less critical recognition than those already discussed but who have never-

theless published significant Jewish fiction include Irvin Faust
(b. 1924), Harvey Swados (1920–1972), Herbert Gold (b. 1924),
Edward Lewis Wallant (1926–1962), Judith Rossner (b. 1935),
Johanna Kaplan (b. 1942), Mark Harris (b. 1922), Irwin Shaw
(b. 1913), Meyer Levin (1905–1981), Cynthia Ozick (b. 1928),
Tillie Olsen (b. 1913), and Grace Paley (b. 1922).

Irvin Faust's stories are an adroit blend of social history
and psychology. His typical protagonist belongs to a New York
minority group and suffers a psychic change (usually dissocia-
tion of personality) in relationship to some upheaval in social
history. The catalyst of change can seem negligible. In the title
story of the collection *Roar Lion Roar* (1965), a Puerto Rican
youth commits suicide because Columbia University loses a
football game, and in the novel *Foreign Devils* (1973), President
Nixon's flight to Peking starts a Jewish novelist on a long road
to self-acceptance. The catalyst of change can also be momentous: in *A Star in the Family* (1975), a Jewish vaudevillian
deteriorates psychologically in response to the assassination of
John F. Kennedy. Whether negligible or momentous, such
events are covert ministers to the spirit in Faust's novels, and
the psychodramas they inspire are staged with insight and
compassion.

An unregenerate child of the 1930s, Harvey Swados continued throughout a prolific career to devote himself to the
novel of social criticism. From the stories of factory life in *On
the Line* (1957), to the tale of three brothers who contend over
a legacy in *The Will* (1963), to the portrait of a socialist cell in
the late 1930s in *Standing Fast* (1970), his novels are unabashedly polemical and committed to the notion that socialism
would improve the workers' lot. As one might expect, characterization is generally superseded by polemic in his novels,
but as social criticism the novels are tough minded and realistic. The single exception to their mode is the posthumously
published *Celebration* (1975), which purports to be the diary of
a man who records only what he doesn't like about himself,
lest he forget who he really is in his much-honored old age. A

study of character more than a social critique, it is ironically the author's finest novel.

Herbert Gold displays a greater virtuosity in his fiction than either Faust or Swados. *The Man Who Was Not With It* (1956), his best known work, is a spirited evocation of a carnival worker's life, while *The Great American Jackpot* (1969), *Swiftie the Magician* (1974), and *Waiting for Cordelia* (1977) are hard-edged satires that focus on California life in the 1960s and 1970s. Written in a softer, almost nostalgic mode, *Therefore Be Bold* (1960), *Fathers* (1967), and *Family* (1981) are loosely autobiographical novels about growing up in Chicago. Gold is an insistent stylist, and his fiction is marked by a Joycean word-play that tends to disjoint his muscular plots and sharply observed detail. If the short stories collected in *Love & Like* (1960) and *The Magic Will* (1971) enjoy more critical acclaim than Gold's novels, it is because they tend less than the novels to be off-balanced by verbal sport.

The premature death of Edward Lewis Wallant was a loss to contemporary literature. His four novels, *The Human Season* (1960), *The Pawnbroker* (1961), *The Tenants of Moonbloom* (1963), and *The Children at the Gate* (1964), are fine, tenebrous studies of blighted human beings who against all odds rediscover the human emotions. *The Pawnbroker* is Wallant's masterpiece. The story of Solomon Nazerman, a survivor of the Nazi concentration camps, it records the slow erosion of Nazerman's anesthetic numbness, and with disquieting intensity it entangles Nazerman in the life of down-and-outers who parade into his shop, particularly in the life of a Puerto Rican named Jesus Ortiz who finally gives his life for Nazerman during a holdup. This parade of junkies, hoodlums, and floaters is a notable feature of Wallant's last three novels. Superficially a danse macabre, it is really a dance of life, a strutting and fretting of poor fools signifying the eternal vitality of the human spirit.

Judith Rossner's *To the Precipice* (1966), *Nine Months in the Life of an Old Maid* (1969), *Any Minute I Can Split* (1972),

Attachments (1977), and *Emmaline* (1980) are a varied lot of novels, but all are fragile barks set tentatively on the dark waters of psychopathology, and all founder on the shoals of characterization. *Looking for Mr. Goodbar* (1975) is Rossner's best novel to date, for it takes intelligent soundings of sexual pathology and creates a substantial character in the person of Theresa Dunn. Enmeshed in a double life, by day a Catholic schoolteacher and by night a barfly, Theresa pursues a course of self-destruction that eventually finds consummation at the hands of a casual lover. The novel is based on the actual murder of a New York City schoolteacher, and though it is clumsy in several respects, it catches well the 1960s dream of sexual free-dom—its appeal, its delusions, and its terrible dangers.

Johanna Kaplan's first novel, a jewel entitled *O My America!* (1980), fulfills admirably the promise of her story collection *Other People's Lives* (1975). The novel's main character is Ezra Slavin, a self-styled "guru to the disaffected young," recently deceased, and his story is told by his second child, Merry, in an effort to counterbalance praise heaped upon the famous man after his death. Merry emphasizes not only the social and po-litical currents that absorbed Slavin's energy, but the emo-tional damage he wreaked upon his wives and children. Kap-lan's sensitivity to nuances of speech and character catches the iconoclastic temperament in full-feathered flight, and her Cook's Tour of Jewish liberalism is as satirically acute as it is superbly funny.

Mark Harris is the author of an engaging baseball trilogy composed of *The Southpaw* (1953), *Bang the Drum Slowly* (1956), and *A Ticket for a Seamstitch* (1957). But Harris rarely strikes any deeper note than geniality, and his failure to tap deeper emotions seems linked to his auctorial temperateness, a matter of straightforward plot construction, low-keyed sty-listics, and modest goals. *Wake Up, Stupid* (1959) is a pleasant experiment in the epistolary form, but it dissipates its satiric energy in farce. *Something about a Soldier* (1957) surrenders the force of its pacifist theme in a similar way, and *Killing Everybody* (1973) probes the mind of a psychopathic murderer only to discover ready-made profundities. Even *Bang the Drum Slowly*, an otherwise adept novel about the death of a young athlete, is disconcertingly easy, its sentiments shopworn and its plot a cliché.

Like Harris, Irwin Shaw is generally thought to have failed his gift. *The Young Lions* (1948), his first and most famous novel, gave evidence of his fine eye for detail and his dramatist's sense of scene, as did the short stories he published in the 1930s and 1940s. *Evening in Byzantium* (1973) and the dynastic diptych *Rich Man, Poor Man* (1970) and *Beggarman, Thief* (1977) continue to evidence Shaw's enormous technical expertise, but even these best of his recent novels are potboilers—professional potboilers to be sure, astutely paced and interesting in the glimpses they afford of life in international society, but potboilers nonetheless, stylistically pallid and glossily formulaic.

Less natively talented than either Harris or Shaw, Meyer Levin compensates for his lack with indefatigable seriousness. Taking as his special subject the modern history of the Jews, he traces in a series of novels a path that leads from Dachau to Israel, and in the clumsily earnest prose of *My Father's House* (1947), *In Search* (1950), *The Obsession* (1973), and *The Spell of Time* (1974), he enshrines the Zionist impulse as no other American novelist. *The Settlers* (1972) and *The Harvest* (1978), two novels in what seems to have been projected as a dynastic trilogy, complete this Zionist series by tracing the Jewish presence in Palestine up to Israel's emergence as an independent state in 1948.

A trio of women, Cynthia Ozick, Tillie Olsen, and Grace Paley, has brought a special distinction to the Jewish short story. The title story of Ozick's *Bloodshed* (1976) is typical of her work. A "riddle" story, it concerns a young man with ambivalent but violent feelings about the Hassidim who appears before a Hassidic rabbi brandishing two guns, one real and one a toy. The rabbi elects to confiscate the toy, since he thinks the symbolic firearm the more dangerous. The stories in Olsen's *Tell Me a Riddle* (1961) are equally striking, and, like

Ozick's stories, they are filled with quirky intelligence and wit. "Tell Me a Riddle" pits immigrant American Jews against their American-born children, who are more prosperous than they, but discontented and unable to understand the emotions of their aged forebears. Such ironies of life are especially irksome to Olsen's women. Hard-working creatures who measure time by day-old bread, they dream incessantly of some cranny of life they might call their own. Grace Paley tells the story of such women with more humor and optimism. Her stories in *The Little Disturbances of Man* (1959) and *Enormous Changes at the Last Minute* (1974) are not specifically feminist, but Paley's women bring a special jauntiness to life's disruptions, and they are more competent than Ozick's heroines to deal with life's traumas. Increasingly, Paley's stories take on the aura of progressive politics, and increasingly her stories are only sketches—comic monologues that abandon all pretense of narration. Together with Ozick's and Olsen's stories, however, they make an important contribution to the Jewish literature of ethnic sensibility.

BLACK FICTION

If Jewish novels sound a note of alienation from the mainstream culture, black novels constitute a symphony on the subject. Indeed, since 1960 many spokesmen for black writers have claimed that black literature is a separatist art—that a black aesthetic elementally shapes their writing, rendering it a sacred ground not to be trodden critically by nonblacks. Their claim is ill advised, if only because it risks being understood as a whimper of inferiority rather than as a cry of aesthetic independence. Such accomplished black novelists as Ralph Ellison (b. 1914) and James Baldwin (b. 1924) have no need of its evasions.

Ralph Ellison's first and only novel, *Invisible Man* (1952), is a work of art without peer in black fiction. A Bildungsroman that successfully coordinates realism and expressionism, it is the story of a young black man's disillusionment, first with American capitalism, then with socialism, and ultimately with all the clichés of black aspiration. Although very much a novel about discovering one's black identity—that is to say, one's "invisibility"—it traces in symbolic terms the historical range of black experience in America. Its major themes are the betrayal of the race by its alleged champions and the grass-roots development of black anger, but individual chapters might be labeled "slavery," "Tuskegee Institute," "heading north," "unionism," "Marcus Garvey," and "rioting in the streets." Ellison's artistry is awesome. He invents situations with the profligacy of an inexhaustible imagination; his characters live, breathe, and shed real blood; his language dips and soars, howling, whispering, and orchestrating the whole gamut of human feelings. *Invisible Man* is a major achievement not only in black fiction but in the American novel.

Although James Baldwin has never fulfilled his early promise, his commitment to his writing and the prestige he enjoys are considerable. *Go Tell It on the Mountain* (1953) is his first and most striking novel. The story of a fourteen-year-old's conversion in a storefront church in Harlem, it is an ironical *J'accuse* that indicts the American system for offering black youth only primitive Calvinism (or drugs, or alcohol) as a substitute for the American Dream. Baldwin's subsequent novels invoke kindred themes of racial and sexual oppression, but they are less carefully shaped than his first. *Giovanni's Room* (1956), *Tell Me How Long the Train's Been Gone* (1968), *If Beale Street Could Talk* (1974), and *Just above My Head* (1979) are competent works, but undistinguished. Among Baldwin's later novels, only *Another Country* (1962), with its vision of racial and sexual bigotry overcome, can lay claim to critical importance. Baldwin's reputation today is increasingly dependent on his essays. Collected in *Notes of a Native Son* (1955), *Nobody Knows My Name* (1961), *The Fire Next Time* (1963), and *The Devil Finds Work* (1976), they are major texts in the literature of black liberation and significant memoranda to the nation's conscience.

A number of black writers stand in the shadow of Ellison and Baldwin but nevertheless command an interracial and sometimes international audience. Chester Himes (b. 1909), John A. Williams (b. 1925), Ernest J. Gaines (b. 1933), Toni Morrison (b. 1931), and Ishmael Reed (b. 1938) are most prominent among them, but many others might be cited—Henry Van Dyke (b. 1928), Charles S. Wright (b. 1932), and Clarence Major (b. 1936), who have done significant work in the fabulistic mode, as well as Ann Petry (b. 1911), Owen Dodson (b. 1914), William Demby (b. 1922), William Gardner Smith (1926–1974), Julian Mayfield (b. 1928), and Alice Walker (b. 1944). In many ways the most powerful writing by blacks has been in autobiography and its derivative forms, notably Richard Wright's (1908–1960) extraordinary *Black Boy* (1945), Eldridge Cleaver's (b. 1935) *Soul on Ice* (1968), Theodore Rosengarten's (b. 1944) compilation *All God's Dangers: The Life of Nate Shaw* (1974), and Alex Haley's (b. 1921) *Roots* (1976).

Chester Himes began his long and prolific career writing tendentiously angry novels about racism in the defense plants of Los Angeles during World War II. Three autobiographical novels followed, all of them somewhat overstuffed and melodramatic. In such camp detective novels as *The Real Cool Killers* (1959), *All Shot Up* (1960), and *Cotton Comes to Harlem* (1965), Himes found his fictional stride. Detectives "Coffin" Ed Johnson and "Gravedigger" Jones attempt to dispense a crude justice, but Harlem is beyond civil control, and the merely hateful environment of Himes's early novels becomes surrealistic chaos in these divertissements, a madhouse whose shatterpated inmates have to contend with invincible anarchy. Exuberantly camp, *Pinktoes* (1961) is a bawdy satire about middle-class blacks and liberal whites who go to bed together to promote racial understanding. It enjoys a cult reputation in both the United States and France.

The novels of John A. Williams mirror the changing focus of black anger. *The Angry One* (1960), *Night Song* (1961), and *Sissie* (1963) are integrationist stories, and *The Man Who Cried I Am* (1967), *Sons of Darkness, Sons of Light* (1969), and *Cap-*

tain Blackman (1972) are militantly apocalyptic fictions that do not hesitate to imagine racial civil war and an international conspiracy to exterminate the black race. *Mothersill and the Foxes* (1975), *The Junior Bachelor Society* (1976), and *!Click Song* (1982) are more sanguine works, less stridently racial. An accomplished writer in the realistic mode, Williams is a master of characterization and likes to confront his protagonists with imminent crises, forcing them to review and reevaluate their past lives. If this is a recognizable formula in his novels, it is an elastic formula that he employs with originality and force.

Ernest J. Gaines has proven himself less ready than Williams to accommodate his art to rhetorical fashions. Essentially a naturalist and something of a latter-day Faulkner, he sets his novels in an imaginary "Bayonne" region of Louisiana's bayou country. After two apprentice novels, he served up a fine collection of short stories in *Bloodline* (1968); a dazzling, hundred-year saga of rural Louisiana blacks in *The Autobiography of Miss Jane Pittman* (1971); and a probing account of the rupture between a black preacher and his radicalized son in *In My Father's House* (1978). *The Autobiography of Miss Jane Pittman* is an especially fine novel, rich in incident and artfully evocative of the oral traditions of narrative. Jane Pittman herself, a black woman whose life spans both slavery and the civil-rights movement, is one of the memorable characters of contemporary American fiction.

Toni Morrison's four novels shine brightly in the literary firmament, several of them with a feminist spark. *The Bluest Eye* (1970) is the story of a young black girl who wants blue eyes so that she can be beautiful and happy; *Sula* (1973) traces the friendship of two black girls; and *Tar Baby* (1981) is a story of race and motherhood. The most critically acclaimed of Morrison's novels is *Song of Solomon* (1977). The story of a black man's exploration of his family history and his discovery that history fades into myth, it is shot through with the fantastical events and intricate symbolism that are the author's trademark. Morrison's narrative strategies are brilliantly experimental, and her prose is a lively blend of dialectical ebullience and biblical allusiveness. "It's always seemed to me black people's grace has been what they do with language," she once remarked. Not an easy writer, she is nevertheless an accessible one, and her delight in her black sensibility is unstrained.

Although Ishmael Reed affects to be governed by a specifically black aesthetic, his exaggerated parodies, his cartoon-like characters, and his esoteric allusiveness are staples of contemporary absurdist fiction. Indeed, Reed is essentially a parodist. *The Free-Lance Pallbearers* (1967) is a parody of the black Bildungsroman; *Yellow Back Radio Broke-Down* (1969) is a parody of the Western dime novel; *Mumbo Jumbo* (1972) and *The Last Days of Louisiana Red* (1974) are parodies of detective thrillers; *Flight to Canada* (1976), his best novel, is a parody of the escaped-slave narratives popular in nineteenth century America; and *The Terrible Twos* (1982) is a parody of many things, but especially the St. Nicholas legend. Reed overloads his fictions with Vodoun and Egyptian esoterica in his attempt to give them a black provenance, but his iconoclastic humor cuts through his allusiveness without missing a comic beat. His language—a blend of academic jargon and one-liners—is a jazzily energetic performance.

WESTERN FICTION

The work of contemporary Western writers is less self-consciously a component of American literature than that of Southern, Jewish, and black writers, but it is an emerging school of fiction that may yet rout the saddle-worn pieties of Zane Grey. The new Western writers tend to explore contemporary realities: the West's fragile balance of Indians, Hispanics, and Anglos; its legacy of ecological unconcern; its perennial but empty promise to those in search of El Dorado. "The West is a wreck," says the novelist Thomas McGuane in a stance typical of contemporary Western writers; "I'd like to document that without getting totally depressing about it." Technically

a Midwesterner, Wright Morris (b. 1910) has deep affinities
with the Western writers and is in some ways their dean. William Eastlake (b. 1917), William Humphrey (b. 1924), and
Larry McMurtry (b. 1936) figure prominently in the literature
without quite dominating it. Other important writers include
Edward Abbey (b. 1927), John Nichols (b. 1940), and the Native
Americans N. Scott Momaday (b. 1934), James Welch (b. 1940),
and Leslie Marmon Silko (b. 1948).

In the course of his long career, Wright Morris has set
novels in many parts of the world, but he has set them most
often in his native Nebraska. A photographer as well as a novelist, he has also published important photographic studies of
the Midwest, and reading Morris's novels is like turning the
pages of those photographic studies: a series of static scenes
conveys in both media a sense of life beaten into subjection by
an outsize landscape. Distances are an invitation to despair,
human artifacts are emblems of failure, and all towns except
Chicago are ghost towns. *The Field of Vision* (1956) and *Ceremony in Lone Tree* (1960) are Morris's most accomplished novels. Typically, they emphasize characterization and depict aged
Nebraskans who have so lost the taste for life that they simply
record the things they see, as if themselves cameras. The past
mocks them with its unfulfilled promises, and the future mocks
them with lowering violence. The present holds only their cam-
era eye, which focuses where the sentimental and the comedic
intersect.

A New Yorker by birth, William Eastlake did not settle
in New Mexico until the early 1950s, but the apparent timelessness of the desert landscape immediately captured his
imagination. Transforming the New Mexico region into the
fictional Checkerboard of his four Southwestern novels, he
combines a lyrical celebration of the land and its Indian in-
habitants with a deft satire of Anglo venality. Eastlake's
themes are large ones: time and timelessness, death and resurrection, life and art, fidelity and treachery. *Go in Beauty*
(1956), his highly regarded first novel, is the story of a writer
who tries unsuccessfully to separate himself from his Check-

erboard homeland. *The Bronc People* (1958) is even more highly regarded—a fine novel about a conflict between blacks and whites as observed and manipulated by Indians. The New Mexican setting is not just decor in this novel but a perspective on the narrative action, and in a masterful illusion of Eastlake's art the desert, mesa, and sky seem to hold humanity up to judgment. *Portrait of an Artist with Twenty-six Horses* (1963) is less successful, but it is an incisive tale that charts the episodic reminiscences of a man slowly sinking into quicksand. *Dancers in the Scalp House* (1975) is a more conventional story of beleaguered Indians who try to stop their land from being flooded by the government.

Eastlake has also written three war novels. *Castle Keep* (1965) is a World War II story based on Eastlake's own experiences; *The Bamboo Bed* (1969) is a graphic novel about the Vietnam war; and *The Long Naked Descent into Boston* (1977) is a farcical tale that likens the Revolutionary War to the Vietnam involvement. The moon landings are thrown in for comic good measure. Eastlake is one of the better novelists writing today, sometimes unsuccessful but never uninteresting.

Although William Humphrey left his native Texas in the 1940s, that state remains the landscape of his fiction. *Home from the Hill* (1958), *The Ordways* (1965), *A Time and a Place* (1968), and *Proud Flesh* (1973) are all set in the environs of Clarksville in the northeast sector of Texas, and only a few of his early short stories are set elsewhere. *Home from the Hill* dominates Humphrey's output. The story of a young man torn between the ideologies of his sexually promiscuous father and his carefully genteel mother, it reflects Humphrey's abiding concern with the grotesquerie of family life, and like all of his novels, whatever their period, it preserves the Texas of the 1930s in aspic. The language, the folkways, and the general ambience of rural Texas are in fact the strongest appeal of Humphrey's novels, which tend otherwise to constructional weaknesses.

Like Humphrey, Larry McMurtry has left his native Texas but continues to place his writings there, most often in Houston and the fictional town of Thalia. *Horseman, Pass By* (1961) and *Leaving Cheyenne* (1963), his first novels, are stories about the enforced contiguity of people whose temperaments are profoundly mismatched. Somber but tightly woven fictions, they augured a career deflected by McMurtry's sudden preference for more loosely constructed narrative. *The Last Picture Show* (1966) is the first and most successful of his novels in this looser mode. Focusing on three teenagers who are as mismatched as everyone else in McMurtry's novels, it relieves its cheerless metaphysic with their adolescent pratfalls. *Moving On* (1970), *All My Friends Are Going to Be Strangers* (1972), and *Terms of Endearment* (1975) also employ comic relief, but characterization and the occasional set piece seem their entire strength.

Edward Abbey and John Nichols seem less concerned with evoking the landscape and cultures of the Southwest and more concerned with ecological preservation. In the autobiographical *Desert Solitaire* (1968) and *Black Sun* (1971) Abbey has posed difficult questions about man's earthly stewardship, and in *The Monkey Wrench Gang* (1975) and *Good News* (1980) he has propounded the same questions in brashly extravagant satire. Nichols has published a comic trilogy set in Chamisaville, a fictionalized version of Taos, New Mexico. *The Milagro Beanfield War* (1974), *The Magic Journey* (1978), and *The Nirvana Blues* (1981) depict the evolution of Chamisaville from a sleepy village into a tourist spot exploited by local Anglos at the expense of the Chicano and Indian populations. Nichols is too much the preacher in these novels, but he is a lively satirist with an engaging affection for rural silliness. *A Ghost in the Music* (1979), a son's appreciation of a father too big for life, is his most impressive novel.

Native American writing is slowly coming into its own. N. Scott Momaday, who is a Kiowa Indian, has set down the legends of his tribe with great dignity in *The Way to Rainy Mountain* (1969) and has suggested the Native American sensibility in several volumes of poetry. *House Made of Dawn* (1968), his single novel, fully merits the Pulitzer Prize it was awarded in 1969. James Welch, half Blackfoot and half Gros Ventre, is the author of two distinguished novels, *Winter in the Blood* (1974) and *The Death of Jim Loney* (1979), both concerned with modern-day Indians who have lost their sense of identity. Leslie Marmon Silko, who was raised on a Pueblo reservation in New Mexico, has written with originality and assurance about the Laguna. She blends prose narrative with verse in her novel *Ceremony* (1978) and in her miscellany *Storyteller* (1981).

THE BEATS

Writers not ethnocentrically based have also made dispossession and alienation their subject. The neo-Romantic Beat movement, for instance, sponsored a mystique of sex, drugs, love, jazz, and anarchy to express a minority discontent in the 1950s with the American esteem for progress and power. What originated as naturalist observation of society's underbelly evolved into visionary expression of a more individualist and personal American—a BEATific vision, according to Jack Kerouac (1922–1969), who was the movement's most important novelist.

There is some truth to Leslie Fiedler's suggestion that the poet Allen Ginsberg created Jack Kerouac, but it is no less true that Kerouac created himself in a series of confessional novels he privately called "The Legend of Duluoz." Ultimately, "Duluoz" and the other Kerouac personas in these novels are in quest of heroes—persons who retain their individuality and self-determination in the context of postwar conformity. To a limited extent, these questers are already the heroes they seek, for setting out on the road is for them a heroic choice not to interfere with the self-determination of others. "Beat" themselves (in the sense of beat-down), they add as little as they can to the beat-downedness of others and thereby achieve BEATitude.

On the Road (1957), *The Dharma Bums* (1958), and *The Subterraneans* (1958) are the best of Kerouac's eighteen published books. They are examples of what he called "spontaneous prose," a nonstop flow of narration that is host to every mystical and ecstatic urge as well as to the mundanely picaresque. Kerouac's intention was to "sketch the flow that already exists intact in mind," and "flow" itself was effectively his aesthetic. Memorably emblazoned in his metaphor of the road, "flow" is simply the ongoingness of time and experience—that to which one returns after ecstasy fails. There is something invincibly sweet about Kerouac's Beat mystique and something guileless about his "rucksack revolution," but the best of his novels are apt to survive in the literary histories because they played midwife to the more hardened disenchantments of the 1960s. Less celebrated Beat novelists, such as Chandler Brossard (b. 1922), R. V. Cassill (b. 1919), John Clellon Holmes (b. 1926), and Alexander Trocchi (b. 1925), lack Kerouac's promise of survival.

In *The Electric Kool-Aid Acid Test* (1968), the journalist Tom Wolfe suggests that Ken Kesey (b. 1935) bridges the 1950s Beats and the 1960s hippies. Kesey's *One Flew Over the Cuckoo's Nest* (1962) is indeed at the point where the curve of one movement changes into that of the other. It is the story of a hustler named Randle McMurphy who avoids work by affecting insanity and finds himself locked in a death struggle with a female automaton who presides over the mental ward where he is incarcerated. Hugely appealing, the novel is a Beat manifesto in its approbation of McMurphy's swaggering independence, but a 1960s testament in its conviction that alliances with unreason are necessary if the free spirit is to endure.

Partially subsumed by the Beat Generation and partially serving as its patrons, William Burroughs (b. 1914) and Henry Miller (1891–1980) went further than the Beats in their rebellion against American conformity. Immoderation was their ethic; nihilism and hedonism respectively their moods; risk their modus operandi. Together with the Beats, they reinvigorated the confessional mode and wrote about themselves with a candor and an intensity that shocked their contemporaries.

For many years a drug addict, William Burroughs uses his

onetime addiction as a key to the human experience. *Junkie: Confessions of an Unredeemed Drug Addict* (1953), his first novel, is a conventionally lurid tale, but descriptions of the drug experience, particularly its phantasmagorical horrors and atemporal intermittences, point to the distinctive effects of the more unconventional novels *Naked Lunch* (1959), *The Soft Machine* (1961), *The Ticket That Exploded* (1962), and *Nova Express* (1964). Carved somewhat arbitrarily out of one long manuscript, these four novels have no consistent narrative or point of view, but rather blocks of images linked by theme. Passages of hallucinatory experience interrupt their flow like a persistent tremor, and syntax takes second place to intensity. In several of these novels and in *Exterminator!* (1973), Burroughs also employs a technique he calls the "cut-up," a process by which he writes conventional statements, cuts them into fragments, and rearranges the fragments into word groups that suggest meaning without actually becoming propositional. His stated goal is to cure us of our addiction to preformulated images and syntax and to expand our range of linguistic awareness—our awareness, too, of that silence on the other side of language. Like Tristan Tzara and the surrealists, who conducted similar experiments with verbal sequence, Burroughs seems to lose control of his material on occasion, and he therefore tends to alienate literary traditionalists. *The Wild Boys* (1971), a futuristic but relatively accessible novel about a homosexual tribe of hashish smokers, is the only one of his novels to enjoy widespread critical esteem.

Although Henry Miller belongs chronologically to the generation of writers dominated by Hemingway, Steinbeck, and Dos Passos, his most important novels, *Tropic of Cancer* (1934) and *Tropic of Capricorn* (1939), were victims of censorship in the United States until the early 1960s when Grove Press led a battle to overturn the ban on their publication. Barely fictionalized autobiography, the novels reflect the life Miller experienced and imagined in Paris and New York. More than that, they are uninhibited *jeux d'esprit*—sexually graphic, Rabelaisianly comic, altogether engaging blends of self-mockery and self-promotion. Miller's hero happily embraces poverty and hunger in a celebration of personal freedom. A sensualist, he especially celebrates the visceral, and his story is a hymn to sensuous abandonment, crammed with the sights, sounds, smells, touches, and tastes of Paris and New York. Miller's subsequent novels also tend to shape themselves as a *recherche du temps perdu*, but they flow less euphorically than the Tropic novels, and their celebration of personal freedom tends to be diluted with the sermons of a self-conscious culture hero. *The Rosy Crucifixion*, a trilogy composed of the novels *Sexus* (1949), *Plexus* (1953), and *Nexus* (1960), lacks the vitality of the Tropic novels and is generally thought tedious and uninspired. If Miller's reputation today is inflated by his role in the battle against censorship, his legacy is nonetheless important, especially his emphasis on the autobiographical narrator and his capacity to subsume all experience.

METAFICTION

The most exciting and interesting fiction in the postwar period has little to do with ethnic perspective. It is a surrealistic and fabulistic body of writing that grows out of international modernism with some nourishment from the European Absurdists, the Southern Gothicists, and the New York and California Beats. Stressing the *composed* aspect of fiction, it tends to put in the foreground both language and authorship in an attempt not simply to undercut the illusions of realism but to discover new modes of narrative gamesmanship. Essentially, it is a body of fiction about the making of fictions—political fictions, delusional fictions, narrative fictions; indeed, every kind of fiction.

Not greatly concerned with accessibility, writers of this school tend to repudiate conventions of the well-made novel. "I began to write fiction," says John Hawkes, "on the assumption that the true enemies of the novel were plot, character, setting, and theme, and having once abandoned these familiar ways of thinking about fiction, totality of vision or structure was really all that remained." "The literature of exhaustion," John Barth calls such writing, drawing attention to its cannibalizing reflexiveness. "Surfiction," Raymond Federman calls it, linking it to the surrealists' notion that life itself is a fiction. "Fabulation" is the term Robert Scholes prefers, emphasizing its incorporation of fabulistic didacticism. Underscoring its attempt to transcend narrative orthodoxy, William H. Gass calls it "metafiction."

Whatever one calls it, this experimental writing found its first major novelists in John Hawkes (b. 1925), William Gaddis (b. 1922), and Vladimir Nabokov (1899–1977). When John Barth (b. 1930), William H. Gass (b. 1924), and Thomas Pynchon (b. 1937) joined their distinguished company, a movement was born—one of the most important in the contemporary period. Metafictionists of the second rank include Donald Barthelme (b. 1931), Kurt Vonnegut, Jr. (b. 1922), Richard Brautigan (b. 1935), Thomas McGuane (b. 1939), Gilbert Sorrentino (b. 1929), and Ronald Sukenick (b. 1932).

The controlled wit and compositional intelligence of John Hawkes continues to dominate the metafictional school of writing. His first novel, *The Cannibal* (1949), is an hallucinatory tale of postwar Germany in which the years 1914 and 1945 interfold and lose their distinction in a disturbing montage of genocide and murder. Hawkes's work has gradually become more accessible than *The Cannibal*, although phantasmagorical violence and suprasubtle technique remain his hallmarks. *The Lime Twig* (1961) has proven his most accessible fiction. A surrealistic thriller set in the world of British horse racing, it blends the terrible logic of dreams with an aesthetic orderliness that chills and elates the reader simultaneously. Love and terror, it suggests, are facets of a single yearning.

Second Skin (1964), which purports to be the memoir of a second-rate Gauguin, introduces a more obviously comic note into Hawkes's fiction. This note continues in *The Blood Oranges* (1971) and *Travesty* (1976), but not in *Death, Sleep & the Traveler* (1974), a terrifying novel about an artist who channels his creative power into erotic nightmares in order to satisfy unconscious needs. Elegant, subtle, shot through with parallel images and cross-referencing verbal patterns, *Death, Sleep & the Traveler* is in many ways Hawkes's finest work. *The Passion Artist* (1979) and *Virginie: Her Two Lives* (1982) continue to probe the dark orchestrations of sexual power.

William Gaddis's *The Recognitions* (1955) is one of the cult novels of metafiction—a dazzling tour de force, encyclopedic and esoteric, that depicts a world of elaborately compounded forgeries. Wyatt Gwyon, the central character, gives up plans for the priesthood to become a forger of Flemish Old Masters in a bizarre quest for authentic experience, and at the end of the novel he withdraws to a Spanish monastery to scrape old masterworks down to the canvas in an effort to reach the tabula rasa beyond all fictions. With only slightly less esoterica, *JR* (1975) chronicles the rise and fall of J. R. Vansant, a sixth-grader who parlays his way seriocomically to implausible eminence in the world of high finance. Even more than *The Recognitions, JR* offers the reader an impenetrable linguistic surface. Jargon, clichés, and barbarisms of all kinds proliferate as if out of control, and elephantine dialogues utterly swamp the narrative line. The novel suggests that we are continually victimized by such linguistic fictions and that our ideational constructions have no relevance to the world we hypothesize as real. Like Hawkes, Gaddis proffers aesthetic pleasures as tentative compensation for this Donnybrook Fair of experience.

Born into a distinguished family in Czarist Russia, Vladimir Nabokov adopted America as his homeland in 1940 and transformed himself midway through his life into an Anglo-American novelist. "Riddles with elegant solutions," he once called his densely playful novels, and *Lolita* (1955), *Pnin* (1957), and *Pale Fire* (1962), his three most famous works, are distinguished by convolutions of wit, trilingual puns, and plots that stand acrobatically on their heads. *Lolita* was a succès de scandale—the story of a middle-aged émigré named Humbert Humbert and his erotic obsession with Lolita Haze, the barely pubescent but sexually precocious daughter of his landlady.

Pnin, a succès d'estime, is a comedy of academic politics as experienced by a lovably ineffectual Russian scholar dropped by fate in a thinly disguised version of Cornell University.

Pale Fire is Nabokov's masterpiece. At the novel's center is a heartfelt poem called "Pale Fire" written by the imaginary poet John Shade. Utterly overwhelming the poem are an introduction and a set of loopy notes which argue that the poem is really the life story of Shade's self-appointed editor, Charles Kinbote, who believes himself the deposed King of Zembla. It is finally unclear whether Shade is Kinbote's fantasy, or Kinbote Shade's, but their exuberant mirroring renders the novel a giddy interplay of styles, sensibilities, and sexualities. Nabokov is not without compassion, despite this richly parodic glitter. In Shade-Kinbote, as in all such Nabokovian eccentrics, one is compelled to recognize that obsession is the poetry of a troubled spirit. What is a madman, asks John Shade, but a fellow poet?

John Barth's delight in the hyperbolic is as great as Nabokov's. His first novels, *The Floating Opera* (1956) and *The End of the Road* (1958), were basically realistic fictions informed by black humor—"nihilistic fictions," Barth once called them—but with *The Sot-Weed Factor* (1960) and *Giles Goat-Boy* (1966), Barth allowed his imagination freer play. The first is an epical tale of Ebenezer Cooke, a Poet Laureate of the Maryland Colony who flourished in the first decade of the eighteenth century. Barth's conceit is to imagine Cooke's story in the mode of an eighteenth-century novel with a full measure of whores, highwaymen, and charlatans, with even a delicately incestuous sibling relationship. *Giles Goat-Boy* is as winningly camp. "A souped-up Bible" in Barth's intention, it chronicles the efforts of its title character, the unnatural offspring of a woman and a computer, to preach his Revised New Syllabus at New Tammany College. In *Lost in the Funhouse* (1968) and *Chimera* (1972), Barth turns to short stories, and in interlocked sequences he explores the origins and limits of narrative with his customary penchant for making simple relationships complicated and conventional relationships bawdy. *Letters* (1979), the most hypertrophied of his fictions, is an epistolary novel composed of eighty-eight letters exchanged among seven correspondents loosely connected to *The Sot-Weed Factor*. *Sabbatical* (1982) is a novel so dauntingly solipsistic as to suggest self-parody.

More than any other American writer, Barth makes light of the introspective mood that dominates contemporary art and criticism. Resolutely whimsical, inflexibly frivolous, he turns the existential angst of such introspection into balletic flights of inconsequence. Among the incidental pleasures of his fiction is the tendency of self-conscious grammatical correctness to back his narrators into the odd linguistic corner, but among the transcendent delights of his fiction is a sense of liberation from all such mean entrapment.

A philosopher of language by training, William H. Gass emphasizes in both his fiction and his essays that language has no essential connection with reality. *Omensetter's Luck* (1966), his first novel, is the story of Brackett Omensetter and the impact of his preternatural goodness on a clergyman who retreats into verbalism as if it were a stronghold of reality. Yet victories of the verbal imagination are the only possible victories in Omensetter's world, and to reinforce that theme, Gass brings a mandarin control to his astonishing play of language—densely clotted images, obscene limericks, chiseled dialogue, echoes of the Bible and of the *Farmer's Almanac*. The stories in *In the Heart of the Heart of the Country* (1968) also depict characters who deploy language as a barricade against reality's emptiness. The title story employs titled blocks of statement to describe various aspects of a small Midwestern town and the narrator's life, and in an artful conjunction of the story's form and metaphysic, these blocks of statement are used by the narrator to build a sense of himself. The most radically experimental of Gass's fictions is *Willie Masters' Lonesome Wife* (1968), a novel that uses photographs, a variety of typefaces, and pages of different colors and textures to emphasize that the reading of fiction is preeminently a sensuous experience.

Although he was Nabokov's student at Cornell, Thomas

Pynchon is concerned not at all with the elegance of life's cryptograms, but rather with their terror. Obsessed with the detritus of contemporary civilization, he pits his characters against a mixture of scientific esoterica and sociological absurdity only to torture them with suspicions that the mixture conceals a key that might somehow reverse the tendency of all systems to run down in accordance with thermodynamic law. Each of his three novels takes the shape of a search. *V.* (1963) is the story of Benny Profane and his search for an elusive Mata Hari through proliferating avatars of her being. *The Crying of Lot 49* (1966) is the story of Oedipa Maas and her attempt as an executrix to clarify the octopus holdings of Pierce Inverarity, her onetime lover. *Gravity's Rainbow* (1973) is the story of Tyrone Slothrop and his attempt to discover why he is sexually aroused by the approach of rockets. Unlike Nabokov and Hawkes, Pynchon seems to disbelieve in the power of the mind to shape experience to its private satisfaction, even in the province of his art. Thus, the lines of search in his novels are so complicated by indirection and obscurity, by metaphors hopelessly in search of referents and by erudition hopelessly in search of focus, that their final gestalt is mania. Cartoonstrip comedy adds its peculiar frenzy to this mania, and a singularly lumpish syntax seems to say in its own way that all is dross.

Donald Barthelme is an eminent figure among those writers who attempt to simulate the disjunction of words and things in our civilization and to relate that disjunction to the regenerative powers of the imagination. His short stories, collected under such titles as *Come Back, Dr. Caligari* (1964) and *Unspeakable Practices, Unnatural Acts* (1968), and his novels *Snow White* (1967) and *The Dead Father* (1975) are riddled with incongruities of reference and situation, and sometimes with incongruities of genre as well. In "Me and Miss Mandible" (1966), a grown man finds himself suddenly a student in the sixth grade, and the title character in *Snow White* is a Chinese-American who steps out of Disney and the Brothers Grimm to join a *ménage à huit* in Greenwich Village. Barthelme's genius

is to render such incongruities with an initial whimsy that
fades into desperation. He dramatizes thereby the inability of
an imagination even as dexterous as his to embrace the radically absurd.

"Goddamn it, you've got to be kind," says one of Kurt Vonnegut's characters. Entrapped in a mix of black humor, surrealistic effects, and science fiction, his characters emit such
cries as if they were the last human beings to know virtue.
Less tragic than comedic, they try to live seriously amid the
complications of technology and nonlinear time, but they are
rendered by their author with relentless whimsy, as if whimsy
were apology for his vision of their circumstances.

The Sirens of Titan (1959), *God Bless You, Mr. Rosewater*
(1965), and *Slaughterhouse-Five* (1969) promise to be the most
enduring of Vonnegut's novels. "I love you sons of bitches," says
Mr. Rosewater to science fiction writers in the mass. "You're
the only ones who'll talk about the *really* terrific changes going
on . . . the only ones with guts enough to *really* care about the
future, who *really* notice what machines do to us. . . ." Such is
Vonnegut's conceit. Tragic-minded, yet content to be a senti-
mentalist, he appeals enormously to the young in heart. Those
of more hardened sensibility find him insubstantial.

Richard Brautigan is a Beat writer turned *faux naif*. An
early influence of the Beats is evident in his work, particularly
in its attitude toward women, but Brautigan's distinctive note
is a 1960s nostalgia for a more humanly focused America than
he discovers in the wrecking yards and train stations of his
fiction. In tribute to the imaginative largesse of that lost America, Brautigan's novels are written in an offhand style, syn-
tactically laconic and crazily hyperbolic. His genre is often a
derivative of the tall tale—the fishing yarn in *Trout Fishing
in America* (1967), the Gothic Western in *The Hawkline Monster* (1974), the California detective story in *Dreaming of Bab-
ylon* (1977). *Trout Fishing in America* and *The Tokyo-Montana
Express* (1980) are Brautigan's most impressive fictions. Like
all his novels, they affect a disingenuous level of technique as
if to defuse a satiric cartooning that is their real distinction.

But Brautigan coyly misleads us with such strategies. His sweetness cloys and turns claustrophobic, and its collapse in his best work unmasks the face of despair. Too easily dismissed as an out-of-date flower child, he is not Thoreau's disciple but Mark Twain's.

Thomas McGuane is also a disciple of Mark Twain, and in his first three novels he proves himself an adroit comedian with a swaggering irreverence for the American scene. He proves himself an accomplished craftsman as well, inasmuch as *The Sporting Club* (1969), *The Bushwacked Piano* (1971), and *Ninety-Two in the Shade* (1973) are built with a master's steadiness, sentence to paragraph to page. *Ninety-Two in the Shade*, McGuane's most accomplished novel, is a story about two fishing guides in the Florida Keys, one of whom murders the other in retaliation for a practical joke. Taut, mordantly comic, it is classically American in its concern with virility. With *Panama* (1978), McGuane returns to fiction after several years of writing screenplays for Hollywood. Less comically than in his earlier novels, he tells the story of a young celebrity whose mind has been destroyed by the excesses of a meteoric career. "The most sleazed-out man in America," the protagonist calls himself, and a more disorienting plunge than his into the world of sleaze is hard to imagine. In *Nobody's Angel* (1982) McGuane's subject is the new Old West—his style, amusingly laconic once again.

"I'm interested in surfaces and flashes, episodes . . ." says Gilbert Sorrentino, and in a series of novels he has refined a pointillist technique based on brief, crystalline scenes. All of his novels are difficult, but ease of access is not the point in Sorrentino's aesthetic creed. Totality of effect, however, *is* the point, and arrays of flashing scenes configure shapes in his novels without delimiting a narrative line. Each novel configures something different. *The Sky Changes* (1966) presents a foundering marriage; *Steelwork* (1970) evokes a Brooklyn neighborhood in the late 1930s and the 1940s; *Imaginative Qualities of Actual Things* (1971) surveys the avant-garde art world of the 1960s; and *Splendide-Hôtel* (1973) offers twenty-six prose poems, alphabetically generated, that mix fiction and literary criticism. *Mulligan Stew* (1979) is Sorrentino's masterpiece. A vast, hugely allusive novel, it is a stylistic panoply that incorporates imitations of the Jewish novel, the Western saga, pornographic fiction, and the detective story, to list only a few of its comic turns. As pointillist paintings convey the play of refracted light with special verve, Sorrentino's verbal pointillism catches expertly the play of refracted styles.

Ronald Sukenick is another respecter of surfaces, a believer that "the truth of the page is on top of it, not underneath." In his short fiction "What's Your Story" (1960), Sukenick sits at his desk trying to write a thriller, but the writerly process is inexorably foregrounded. Like Barth's "Life-Story" (1968) and Barthelme's "Sentence" (1970), the work is ultimately a nonstory about the writer's relationship with his imagination. Sukenick continues to uphold the primacy of imagination and language in several antinovels, notably *Out* (1973), a story about leaving New York's Lower East Side for California in the hot flash of the 1960s. As the author gradually walks "out" on the novel and its dead-end logistics, interlinear spacing grows entropically until the print disappears and whiteness spreads over the page. Sukenick's best novel, *98.6* (1975), is also concerned with the 1960s counterculture—specifically, with its search for a 98.6 norm of spiritual health. A documentary collage in the first third of the novel is not successful, but as Sukenick's characters fade into oblivion, imagination and language survive them, even an imaginary language called Bjorsq. Sukenick seems determined to open up possibilities of literary play not yet current in our texts.

Writers less boldly experimental than Barthelme, Sorrentino, and Sukenick sometimes employ metafictional techniques in the service of traditionally illusionistic fiction. Although metafiction involves a radical honesty about narrative illusions, its blending with illusionism produces effects not so much bizarre as intense. These effects are often superior to the results of the more radically experimental writers. The most distinguished of these temperate metafictionists are Jerzy Kosinski (b. 1933), James Purdy (b. 1923), Robert Coover (b. 1932), John Irving (b. 1942), and Joan Didion (b. 1934).

Born in Poland of Russian parents, Jerzy Kosinski came to America in 1957. His writings are entirely in English, both his pseudonymous sociological writings and the novels he publishes under his real name. "I was never at home in my native country," he has said; "therefore I am never at home in my native tongue." Kosinski's first novel, *The Painted Bird* (1965), concerns the wanderings of a homeless boy through Eastern Europe during World War II. Its Kafkaesque horrors are based on Kosinski's actual experiences but seem mordantly surrealistic, and it has proven Kosinski's most affecting novel. *Steps* (1968), *The Devil Tree* (1973), *Cockpit* (1975), *Blind Date* (1977), *Passion Play* (1979), and *Pinball* (1982) employ the same flickering scenes of violence and fantasy-violence that are startling in *The Painted Bird*, but they do so in a less compassionate context. *Steps* is the best of Kosinski's fictions. In a series of discontinuous passages related with icy unfeelingness, its unnamed narrator establishes terrible connections between what he has seen and what he is—the "steps" of undigested experience that have shaped his potential for evil. This shaping of a potential for evil is Kosinski's great subject. He is not a lover of the grotesque and the macabre for their own sake, but a sociological moralist, fascinated by the traumatized ego that must test its control by injecting large measures of odium into its anesthetized experience.

James Purdy's fiction has a marked affinity with Kosinski's. His narrators tend to be memoirists who impose the discipline of their narration on stories of violent and traumatic loss, and they tend, like Kosinski's spokesmen, to focus on a situation at its moment of maximum horror. The perversions of Purdy's characters range from incest to sadomasochism to vampirism, and his minor characters often seem dream figures, born not of women but of psychological needs. His prose, sparing of adjectives and adverbs, also recalls Kosinski's, especially when it describes the surrealistically lurid worlds of *Malcolm* (1959) and *I Am Elijah Thrush* (1972). Purdy's most recent fiction is less cluttered with multiple plots and episodes than his earlier fiction, but *The House of the Solitary Maggot* (1974), *In a Shallow Grave* (1976), and *Narrow Rooms* (1978) are still in his accustomed mode—darkly fantastical allegories of eternal children lost in a nightmare universe. Charlatans, psychotics, and unnameable monsters wait to spring in the dark passageways of their minds, and those children who would usurp their lost father's role become monsters themselves, consigned to the Slough of Despond.

In a series of thoughtfully unconventional fictions, Robert Coover suggests our invincible need for the sort of fantasies that trouble Purdy. History, religion, myth, science, mathematics, politics—in Coover's view all are fantasies that soothe the human spirit with taxonomic neatness and specious claims to order. In *The Universal Baseball Association, Inc., J. Henry Waugh, Prop.* (1968), Coover depicts a lonely, middle-aged accountant who invents a baseball league and plays all its games in his head. His fantasy is not his passion alone, but the grand passion of JHWH, whose Tetragammaton echoes with Waugh's name. The disturbing joke of the novel is that Waugh's baseball fantasy survives his death, as creation survives the alleged death of God.

Fantasy's evolution into a self-sufficient reality is also the theme of Coover's *The Public Burning* (1977), a fantastical elaboration of the Rosenberg executions partially narrated by Richard Nixon and climaxed by a "public burning" of the spies in Times Square. Like all Coover's fictions, the novel is marked by a sympathetic understanding of the impulses that lead to dogmatic extremism. As he careens wildly to his destiny at the center of the scapegoat ceremony in Times Square, Nixon simply wants what all Coover's characters want—order, balance, surcease from flux. Such are we all, says Coover, and such is the danger of our psychic life.

John Irving writes about slightly crazed individuals who rely too much on themselves, botch their lives, and reassemble them into insubstantial wholes. Conventional novels of character for the most part, his stories are shaped by melodramatic plot lines and made comfortably lucid by a prose style that prefers clarity to involution and allusion. An old-fashioned spaciousness and a Dickensian array of secondary characters make *The World According to Garp* (1978) and *The Hotel New Hampshire* (1981) especially successful, but a metafictional edge gives all Irving's novels contemporary bite. His elaborate patterning is often without point and has a consequent tendency to seem claustrophobic, to hint at an excessive impingement of imagination on the spaciousness of life. His imaginary writers and his repeated iconography (Vienna, bears, wrestlers) suggest an auctorial foregrounding as interestingly obsessive as Garp's anxiety about his children's safety. With a high-handedness that can only be understood as parodying the traditional novel, Irving arranges fantastical coincidences and ludicrously outsize digressions. Most outrageous of all are his cunning silences. One such silence conceals the death of Garp's younger son and infuriates the reader who has come to depend on Irving's largesse. Something of a trickster, certainly a master of effects, Irving is a comic scourge who menaces us with tragedy.

At a polar extreme from Irving, Joan Didion writes spare, beautifully chiseled novels about broken women playing out the fag ends of their lives. *Run River* (1963) begins with Lily McClellan discovering that her husband has murdered her lover, and the remainder of the novel explains how nineteen years of marriage had come to such a pass. *Play It as It Lays* (1970) chronicles the decline of Maria Wyeth, a sometime actress institutionalized in a mental hospital, who vaguely welcomes apperceptional nothingness. *A Book of Common Prayer* (1977) is the story of Charlotte Douglas, a woman half-drugged with failure, who maintains the standards of life to which she was bred until she meets her death in a Latin American revolution.

The melodrama flaunted in Irving's novels is checked in Didion's by a carefully understated prose—elliptic, terse, pregnant with unstated conclusions. If her main characters are somnambulistic, the totemistic repetition of phrases and an occasional eruption of the grotesque convey a substratum of emotion too painful to be admitted to their feelings. One aches for Charlotte Douglas in her drift toward madness as one aches for what Wallace Stevens called "the unreal of what is real." No one writes a prose more elegantly, ominously honed than Didion's in *A Book of Common Prayer*, and no one tells us with more heartbreaking effect that we are held together by the small, apparently meaningless rituals of life.

A last word might be said about James McCourt (b. 1941), the talented author of a light-as-air novel, *Mawrdew Czgowchwz* (1975). McCourt recounts the career of "the diva of the moment," a woman compounded of several leading singers of the 1940s and 1950s, from her dramatic landing on the Champs-Élysées in a single-engine plane, to her triumphal procession to the old Metropolitan Opera House in New York, to the unfolded secret of her birth. No one has caught in more perfumed amber the mystique of the opera celebrity; no one has rendered more definitively the cult of fanship; few have replicated so well the manner of the English novelist Ronald Firbank. McCourt is representative of many novelists who produce works of art not adequately noticed in the rush of literary fashion. The relative obscurity of *Mawrdew Czgowchwz* reminds us that for every fiction memorialized in the literary histories, hundreds of comparable works go unnoticed.

3 · DRAMA

Although drama in America is the most socially sensitive of the arts, it often seems to thrive on adverse social circumstances. It survived the Great Depression, for instance, surprisingly well. Forced to retrench and centralize, it was also forced to discover a new audience, and by the mid-1930s such organizations as the Theatre Collective and the Group Theatre were performing for audiences that applauded dramas of social awareness as though greeting the dawn of a new age. World War II and its aftermath took an enormous toll from this renaissance. The demise of the Federal Theatre, the rout of the Left, and the near-bankruptcy of Broadway theaters proved dispiriting, and playwrights who had established their reputations before the war suddenly seemed unable to write significant drama, as if their theater had lost its vital force. Maxwell Anderson (1888–1959), S. N. Behrman (1893–1973), Marc Connelly (1890–1980), Moss Hart (1904–1961), George S. Kaufman (1889–1961), Elmer Rice (1892–1967), Robert E. Sherwood (1896–1955), and Thornton Wilder (1897–1975) continued to write new plays, but only a few of their postwar dramas were successful and seem noteworthy today.

Eugene O'Neill (1888–1953) is the single prewar dramatist to make a major impact on the contemporary stage. Six of his plays had their premieres after the war: *The Iceman Cometh* (1946),* *A Moon for the Misbegotten* (1947), *Long Day's Journey*

---

* Unless the context fixes another basis, dates given for plays represent the first American production or the first American publication, whichever is earlier.

into Night (1956), *A Touch of the Poet* (1958), *Hughie* (1964), and *More Stately Mansions* (1967). Of these, *The Iceman Cometh* and *Long Day's Journey into Night* are acknowledged not only as O'Neill's best work but as masterworks of the contemporary theater. Largely on their basis, O'Neill is the most esteemed of American playwrights both in his native land and abroad. Indeed, he is America's only truly international playwright.

The original production of *The Iceman Cometh* in 1946 lacked imagination and made O'Neill's symphonic orchestration of motifs seem tediously repetitious. José Quintero's more sensitive direction of the play in 1956 overcame the forbidding difficulties of its dramaturgy and initiated an O'Neill revival that was intensified a few months later by the premiere of O'Neill's most affecting work, *Long Day's Journey into Night*. A play about familial compassion hard won through suffering, a "play of old sorrow, written in tears and blood," according to O'Neill's description, its distinction is due in part to its autobiographical bloodletting, but due in greater part to its superb theatrics—to its psychological twistings and turnings, its momentary and disconnected illuminations, its elaborate subtext of unspoken feelings, recriminations, and accusations. O'Neill would be important in theatrical history if only for his experiments with dramatic form, but *The Iceman Cometh* and *Long Day's Journey into Night* establish his importance beyond all lines of influence.

BROADWAY

The first major playwrights to emerge after the Second World War are Tennessee Williams (b. 1911) and Arthur Miller (b. 1915). Both dazzled Broadway in the late 1940s, Williams with *A Streetcar Named Desire* (1947), Miller with *All My Sons* (1947) and *Death of a Salesman* (1949). Although they divide the postwar stage between them, two writers could not be more dissimilar. Williams's plays are poetic, evanescent, exotic;

Miller's are prosaic, solidly built, ratiocinative. Yet Miller and Williams are oddly complementary figures in theatrical history. Both helped to commit the American stage to the gutwrenching realism that is its salient characteristic, and both helped to develop a distinctly American mode of tragedy, a tragedy not of great souls, but of persons pathetically ill equipped for life. Their more famous characters have a flesh-and-blood reality beyond that of any characters on the American stage before them, and even the authors' use of expressionistic and symbolistic devices has the paradoxical effect of emphasizing their commitment to realistic drama.

With *Death of a Salesman*, Miller touched America's central nervous system as had few other playwrights. Expressionistic in structure, a "memory play" in design, it overlaps its scenes in atemporal sequence and distills an unforgettable portrait of a salesman who destroys both his family and himself in his devotion to the go-getter gospel. If not profound, *Death of a Salesman* is incisive, and it survives its burden of sententiousness as it survives academic quibbling about whether or not it is a tragedy. Less experimental in form, *The Crucible* (1953) limns a parallel between the Salem witchcraft trials in the seventeenth century and the political excesses of McCarthyism. Its dramatic force has come to outweigh its polemic, and though it has generally been overshadowed by *Death of a Salesman*, it may prove to be Miller's most enduring work.

It is the tragedy of Miller's career that his dramaturgy inexorably weakens as the Leftist sympathy of his early plays evolves into a more profound questioning of social morality. *A View from the Bridge* (1956), *After the Fall* (1964), *Incident at Vichy* (1964), and *The Price* (1968) are replete with guilt and moralistic sociology, but they have less dramatic impact than Miller's earlier plays and a lack of conceptual authority. Afflicted with a moral seriousness too heavy for his talent to bear, Miller becomes more obviously morose in his recent plays, and his indictments of our moral failures become more obviously banal. His position in the theater today is that of an elder statesman.

Tennessee Williams brings to the stage a distinctly Southern sensibility—a penchant for neo-Lawrencian metaphysics and lyricism, a fascination with grotesquerie, and a fondness for characters incapable of dealing with reality. He achieved his first Broadway success in 1945 with *The Glass Menagerie*, the most delicate and in many ways the most appealing of his works. *A Streetcar Named Desire* is sterner melodrama, and the head-on collision of Stanley Kowalski's brutishness with Blanche DuBois's decayed gentility shook Broadway with its power, enshrining itself immediately in American mythology. For almost fifteen years Williams commanded the footlights with a string of such emotionally supercharged plays: *Cat on a Hot Tin Roof* (1955), *Suddenly Last Summer* (1958), *Sweet Bird of Youth* (1959), and *The Night of the Iguana* (1961). In the precarious equilibrium of Williams's art, the strengths of these plays are also their weaknesses. Their surreal psychology is at once trenchant and garish, and their lyricism is at once airborne and melancholic.

Williams's plays since *The Night of the Iguana* fail to achieve this oddly affecting equilibrium. *The Milk Train Doesn't Stop Here Anymore* (1963), *Small Craft Warnings* (1972), *Vieux Carré* (1977), and *Clothes for a Summer Hotel* (1980) rework Williams's familiar themes but with the balance gone, the sentiment become pathos, and the aberrational psychology become frippery. Williams is too much the bohemian to be an elder statesman, but like Miller he is respected today largely for his past achievements.

Dramatists who soothed the hidden fears of Middle America with psychological placebos were Broadway's mainstay in the 1950s. The best of these psychological dramatists was William Inge (1913–1973), and he celebrated an unbroken string of successes in the decade. Robert Anderson (b. 1917), Lillian Hellman (b. 1905), Arthur Laurents (b. 1920), William Gibson (b. 1914), Lorraine Hansberry (1930–1965), Archibald MacLeish (1892–1982), Carson McCullers (1917–1967), Truman Capote (b. 1924), and Paddy Chayefsky (1923–1981) did not have Inge's measure of Broadway success, but like him they were more concerned with sounding the imperatives of human behavior than with orchestrating scenes of heightened confrontation. If they were lowbrow Ibsenites, they offered theatergoers something more substantial than the escapist works that otherwise dominated Broadway—John Patrick's (b. 1906) *The Teahouse of the August Moon* (1953), for instance, or Jerome Lawrence (b. 1915) and Robert E. Lee's (b. 1918) *Auntie Mame* (1956).

William Inge had the opportunity to play Trilby to Tennessee Williams's Svengali but chose the commonplace as his forte rather than Williams's exotica. Drawing on the small-town life of his native Midwest, he glossed the clichés of that life with the clichés of Freudian psychology, and in the cant of the day his themes were existential loneliness, interpersonal alienation, and intrafamilial tension. It is the grace of his plays that Inge shunned such ugly abstractions in favor of dramatic action. Loss and pain do not so much announce as reveal themselves in his work, and they achieve sonority from a hard-surfaced realism that functions as their sounding board. A deeply sentimental writer, he appealed enormously to the temper of the Eisenhower age.

Come Back, Little Sheba (1950) is the first and best of Inge's plays. The story of a desperately lonely husband and wife who reach out tentatively to one another at the final curtain, it is soap opera trimmed of excess sentiment and stiffened with realism. Its final optimism is gratuitous, but cautiously put forth and in no way jarring. In *Picnic* (1953), *Bus Stop* (1955), and *The Dark at the Top of the Stairs* (1957), a note of final optimism sounds more insistently and with less justification, sometimes inanely. The implied reconciliation of Cora and Rubin in *The Dark at the Top of the Stairs* suggests that the bedroom resolves not only incompatible temperaments but economic insolvency.

After this run of successful plays, Inge's career plummeted. *A Loss of Roses* (1959), *Natural Affection* (1963), and *Where's Daddy?* (1966) were justly savaged by the critics, and Broadway theaters were not made available for his last works. His sudden eclipse was due in part to an exhaustion of his themes and in part to the inroads of his personal unhappiness, but due no less to a theater grown weary of easy psychologizing.

Robert Anderson continued to write serious drama through the 1960s and into the 1970s, but he seems linked forever to the 1950s and to his most famous play of the period, *Tea and Sympathy* (1953). Set in a New England boarding school, *Tea and Sympathy* is the story of a sensitive boy, wrongly suspected of being homosexual, and of a housemaster's wife who gives the boy tea, sympathy, and the ultimate assurance of his manhood. "Years from now, when you talk about this . . . and you will . . . be kind" is her well-known line at the last curtain, and kindness is the play's moral focus, even though the homosexual mislabeling might have been a more apposite focus in the McCarthy years.

Except for a fling with comedy in *You Know I Can't Hear You When the Water's Running* (1967) and a fling with overt didacticism in *Solitaire/Double Solitaire* (1971), Anderson has been faithful to his muse and has continued to write plays about the need for human kindness. Lonely people caught in midlife and end-of-life crises reach out to each other in *Silent Night, Lonely Night* (1959), *The Days Between* (1965), and *I Never Sang for My Father* (1968), but with cloyingly sentimental effect. Anderson's best work to date has not been for Broadway but for Hollywood—notably in his screenplay for *I Never Sang for My Father*, which is more disciplined than his play script, more powerful, and more emotionally taut.

Lillian Hellman tends to be grouped with social protest dramatists of the 1930s, but unlike most of those playwrights she was able to accommodate the postwar taste for psychological melodrama. *Another Part of the Forest* (1946), *The Autumn Garden* (1951), and *Toys in the Attic* (1960) replace the one-dimensional characters of her earlier plays with characters psychologically complex, neither wholly good nor wholly evil. At the same time, Hellman continued in her postwar melodramas to demonstrate a mastery of carefully braided plots, labyrinthine complications, and rising lines of action. Indeed, Hellman's craft is so entirely that of the well-made play that it gives off a whiff of old greasepaint and kerosene footlights, not always unpleasantly. But more interesting than her melodramas are two of Hellman's adaptations. *The Lark* (1955) is a nicely Americanized stage piece based on Jean Anouilh's *L'alouette*, and *Candide* (1956) is a piquant and sophisticated treatment of Voltaire's novel. Leonard Bernstein wrote the music for the latter; Richard Wilbur, John Latouche, and Dorothy Parker, the lyrics; Hellman, the maligned book.

Arthur Laurents was excised too readily from the literary histories of Broadway when he began to write librettos. His books for the Leonard Bernstein musical *West Side Story* (1957) and for the Jule Styne musical *Gypsy* (1959) are rightly considered his best works, but Laurents's neglected melodrama is a significant element of the postwar theater. *Home of the Brave* (1945), *The Bird Cage* (1950), *The Time of the Cuckoo* (1952), and particularly *A Clearing in the Woods* (1957) are in many ways more psychologically astute than acclaimed plays that pretend to greater insight. Laurents's failing as a dramatist is his prolixity, an insistence on verbally explicating aspects of his dramatic action better left to suggestion and to the audience's understanding.

William Gibson has published both poetry and fiction, but he established his reputation in the late 1950s with two plays about love as a therapeutic sacrament. *Two for the Seesaw* (1958) is a romantic comedy in which a Jewish girl from the Bronx polishes the rough spots off a WASP lawyer from Nebraska and sends him back to his wife a more understanding man. Vintage Broadway fare, slicked down and weightless, it is nevertheless an amiable work. *The Miracle Worker* (1959) has more substance. A carefully accurate re-creation of Anne Sullivan's tutelage of Helen Keller, it seasons its tribute to love's power with blazing theatrics and a fine sense of the difficulties Sullivan experienced in breaking through Keller's insensibility. Although basically a realistic play, it shifts about freely in time and space and portends the Brechtian theatrics of *Golda* (1978), another "great woman" play that was hopelessly muddled by last-minute rewrites. *A Cry of Players*, written in 1948 but not produced in New York until 1972, suggests the kind of playwright Gibson might have been if psychodrama had not ruled Broadway in the postwar years. The play deals with the young William Shakespeare, whose imagination is fired when a troupe of actors visits his town. It is the play's anachronistic charm that young Will tends to agonize about his call to the boards in a melodious reprise of the plays he was destined one day to write.

A story about a black family living on the South Side of Chicago, Lorraine Hansberry's *A Raisin in the Sun* (1959) is a well-made play in a sentimental mode and an exemplary work of its kind. Tensions wrought by social disadvantage threaten to dismember the family, but the mother's overarching love predictably triumphs, and the ingredients of a classic tearjerker assure that the audience departs the theater handkerchiefs in hand. *A Raisin in the Sun* is of some historical importance, for it is the first play in Broadway history to employ fully rounded black characters. Hansberry's *The Sign in Sidney Brustein's Window* (1964) lacks the cohesiveness of its predecessor but is no less inspirational—a rebuke, in fact, to what its author called "the vogue of unmodified despair" in the work of playwrights like Jean Genet.

At her death a few weeks after the premiere of *The Sign in Sidney Brustein's Window*, Hansberry left unfinished *Les Blancs* (1970), a rebuttal to Genet's *Les Nègres*. Her former husband, Robert Nemiroff, subsequently adapted the play for Broadway. Set in Africa and concerned with the struggle for black liberation, it is a singularly didactic work in its present form, partially redeemed by a cathartic last scene. Nemiroff also assembled *To Be Young, Gifted and Black* (1969), a pastiche of fragments from Hansberry's plays, letters, speeches, and articles. Reverential, too reverential perhaps, its assemblage technique does not flatter Hansberry's writings as much as Nemiroff seems to intend.

Archibald MacLeish is one of several American poets who write drama recognizably in verse, but his *J.B.* (1958) is the only such play to have enjoyed a commercial success on Broadway since the war. A retelling of the Book of Job, *J.B.* has as its setting a traveling circus tarnished with great age. God and the devil are broken-down vendors who preside over contemporary plagues that test the mettle of J.B.'s faith, and at the end of his testing, J.B. discovers—what else?—the human heart. "The candles in the churches are out," his wife concludes in marmoreal doggerel; "The lights have gone out in the sky./ Blow on the coal of the heart/ And we'll see by and by. . . ." *Herakles* (1965), a verse adaptation and updating of Euripides' *Heracles*, is less glittering than *J.B.* in its effects, but less pretentious too, and less second rate in its philosophizing. Tendentious philosophizing is the general failure of MacLeish's drama, not least of all in *Scratch* (1971), a prose play that inflates Stephen Vincent Benét's "The Devil and Daniel Webster" with philosophy. Aesthetically ambitious, but of small theatrical moment, MacLeish's plays are probably destined to be footnotes to his poetry.

Carson McCullers's *The Member of the Wedding* (1950) is a successful play that should have been a failure. Encouraged by Tennessee Williams, but knowing virtually nothing about stagecraft (she had seen only two Broadway plays in her life), McCullers transformed her novel of the same name into an undramatic script that succeeds beautifully on stage despite a lumpish structure and dangerously outsize monologues. The story of an adolescent tomboy who suffers from loneliness and decides to join her brother on his honeymoon, McCullers's play is a fragile, almost unbearably affecting work with a large measure of freshness and psychological probity. Luck, of course, smiles on theatrical naiveté only once: McCullers's second play, *The Square Root of Wonderful* (1957), is as wooden as *The Member of the Wedding* is magically alive.

Truman Capote was not so fortunate as McCullers on Broadway. *The Grass Harp* (1952) lost the tremulous poetry of the author's 1951 novel in its transition to the stage, and Capote's story of a group of people who seek asylum from brute reality by establishing residence in a treehouse proves a leaden idyll in the theater. Like many novelists who attempt to write for Broadway, Capote found it difficult to compose for the actor's voice rather than for the reader's eye. He also experienced difficulty in controlling the tone of his play. Purporting to be fantasy, *The Grass Harp* seems realism gussied up with whimsy, and it suffers in an inevitable comparison with Giraudoux's *The Madwoman of Chaillot*.

Although Paddy Chayefsky achieved more distinction as a scriptwriter for television and motion pictures than as a dramatist, he worked successfully in the theater for more than a decade. His first plays are neat and compact, but too evocative of the small screen that had claimed his earlier allegiance. *Middle of the Night* (1956) is in fact an adapted television drama written according to the model of Chayefsky's television play *Marty* (1953)—a tale of two lonely people who come to love each other despite an urban environment that militates against their love. *The Tenth Man* (1959) is another tribute to love's power, but it is dramaturgically more ambitious—the story of a girl thought possessed who exorcises an unloving spirit from her young man. Gradually, Chayefsky's work moved beyond the sentimental clichés of television and began to depict love as incompatible with self-realization. His hero in *Gideon* (1961), a biblical tour de force set in the year 1100 B.C., demands release from Yahweh's covenant of love: "I cannot love you, God, for it makes me a meaningless thing." "If you love me," he says, "let me believe in mine own self." Gradually Chayefsky embraced a sardonic point of view, tentatively in *The Passion of Josef D.* (1964) and *The Latent Heterosexual* (1968), richly in his filmscripts for *The Hospital* (1971) and *Network* (1976).

Much more than Chayefsky, John Patrick is emblematic of the 1950s American playwright, *species commercialis*. With more than thirty plays to his credit, he has never veered (except once) from sentimentalism, never ceased to affirm the essential goodness of human beings, never failed to be predictable. He enchanted Broadway audiences and proved himself an accomplished craftsman of platitudinous comedy with *The Teahouse of the August Moon* (1953), a story of occupied Okinawa that gently spoofs the American military. *The Hasty Heart* (1945) and *The Curious Savage* (1950) have proved just as durable on the stage.

Patrick is in fact a barometer of mainstream theatrical taste. He wrote successfully for radio theater in its golden age and for Broadway and Hollywood in the fool's-gold fifties, and he has written most recently for the emerging regional and community theaters. Indeed, ever since *Everybody Loves Opal* (1961) failed to take hold on Broadway, Patrick has given the bulk of his new work to theaters outside New York City, and they have had continual success with his light comedies. Patrick's ability to please an ongoing and regenerating audience suggests that the theater of the 1950s has a life span in Middle America that transcends the bounds of its decade.

The success of Frank Gilroy (b. 1925) and Neil Simon (b. 1927) suggests that 1950s drama has an extended life on Broadway as well as in community theaters. It points also to a convergence of television and Broadway, inasmuch as Gilroy wrote for serious dramatic programs like *Playhouse 90* during the 1950s, and Simon was a gag writer for Jackie Gleason, Red Buttons, and other television comedians of the period. It is not generally recognized that the drama of television's golden age imitated the legitimate theater in translating Ibsen and Chekhov into sentimental Freudianism, and it is not generally recognized that situation comedy in the golden age was a close cousin to the Broadway variety, located squarely between satire and farce while carefully avoiding both. With their roots in television and their ultimate success on Broadway, Gilroy and Simon illumine the imitation.

Gilroy's first play, *Who'll Save the Plowboy?* (1962), pulls out every pathetic stop of the 1950s: a terminally ill hero visiting an army buddy whose life he had once saved, a faithless wife, a mongoloid child. His second play, *The Subject Was Roses* (1964), is notable as Broadway's longest-running melodrama of the decade. A thin and sentimental work, the story of a failed marriage whose shallow waters are stirred by a son's return, its dramaturgical pieties found an appreciative audience among those whose sense of theater had been shaped by the small screen.

Neil Simon's plays are as thinly conceived as Gilroy's, but he has parlayed his talent as a gag writer into a more extended success. Indeed, Simon's success is phenomenal, for he virtually dominated Broadway in the 1960s and 1970s and is almost certainly the most financially successful playwright in history. Plotting is not his strength. The unimaginative formula of *Plaza Suite* (1968) is given second life in *California Suite* (1976); and *Barefoot in the Park* (1963), *The Odd Couple* (1965), and *The Sunshine Boys* (1972) elaborate the well-worn formula of two or more characters living in tandem despite radically different temperaments. All these plays are without authority or vision as comic drama, but each is generous with wisecracks and nimble-witted banter. Several have formed the basis of television series, as if they possessed an atavistic homing instinct.

OFF-BROADWAY

Casting her unforgiving eye over postwar Broadway history, Mary McCarthy pronounced in 1958 that the American theater was not only bad, but *very* bad, its plays "horribly badly written." A year later, Gore Vidal complained that love had become noisome in the commercial theater—that it had "replaced the third-act marines of a simpler time." Whatever the incidental excellences and occasional triumphs of postwar Broadway, these observers were justified in their contempt for its standard fare. The commercial plays of the period testify to the cautious temper of the age rather than to the possibilities of theatrical experience.

But while Broadway was growing moribund, off-Broadway theaters were burgeoning in downtown basements and converted lofts. Unlike the commercial theater, the off-Broadway theater was in touch with European influences such as Antonin Artaud's Theater of Cruelty and Samuel Beckett's Theater of the Absurd. It was more attuned than Broadway to the dramaturgy of mime and gesture, and more exploratory of silence and fantasy. Short-lived groups like New Stages and the Abbe Practical Workshop did impressive experimental work and occasionally offered a second chance to plays that had been insensitively produced and critically abused on Broadway. Indeed, O'Neill's *The Iceman Cometh*, Williams's *Summer and Smoke*, and Miller's *The Crucible* were all given their most successful productions off-Broadway.

In the flush of such triumphs, off-Broadway moderated its contempt for the commercial theater and adopted Broadway's hit-or-flop mentality. In turn, Broadway came to view its poor relation not as a rival but as a commercial ally, a useful host for plays that could not be expected to fill the legitimate houses. Still, off-Broadway's tradition of sponsoring experimental drama was not wholly extinguished. In giving stage to the experimental work of Edward Albee (b. 1928), Jack Gelber (b. 1932), Arthur Kopit (b. 1937), Murray Schisgal (b. 1926), and Jack Richardson (b. 1935), off-Broadway spawned some of the most important dramatists of the period.

Edward Albee's first play, *The Zoo Story*, was an unexpected hit when the Provincetown Playhouse produced it in 1960 some months after its premiere in West Germany. Immediately arresting, it is a one-act play in which a man sitting on a park bench is accosted by another man who presses upon him the story of his life. The aggressor finally goads the man into a physical fight, and at the climax of the play he impales himself on a knife he has put into the man's unwilling hand. Absurdist in its plotting, surrealistic in its intensity, realistic in its staging, *The Zoo Story* has the macabre theatricality typical of Albee's best work. In subsequent short plays he has never quite matched its fine modulation of emotion, although *The Sandbox* (1960) and *The American Dream* (1961) bring something of its grisliness to their composite portrait of an American family.

Who's Afraid of Virginia Woolf? (1962) is Albee's masterpiece. A realistic play that depicts an evening in the lives of

two college professors and their wives, it is stuffed to the point
of bursting with confrontational scenes that turn on dialectics
of aggression and impotence, youth and age, reality and illusion. George and Martha, its main characters, express their
love for one another through verbal abuse and through the
shared fantasy that they have engendered a son. These eccen-
tricities trouble the ostensibly normal but more unloving couple, Nick and Honey. As the blackly comic evening builds to
a climax, Albee makes the point that illusions may sustain
marriages (and Western culture) for a period, but there comes
a time to chant a cathartic Dies Irae.

Although it is a less successful play, *A Delicate Balance*
(1966) reprises many of *Virginia Woolf*'s components—the
death of a child, the ambivalence of marital love, the incapacity
of intelligent and educated people to face reality. *All Over*
(1971) repeats many of these ingredients, and like its predecessors it concludes with an elegiac recognition scene that re-
verses its drift toward despair. In the delightful comedy *Sea-
scape* (1975), Albee gives us still another confrontation between
two couples—one human and one ichthyoid.

Critical and popular opinion has turned against Albee in
recent years, discovering in plays from *Tiny Alice* (1964) to *The
Lady from Dubuque* (1980) that borrowings from the European
absurdists conceal an inspirational void and that Albee's word-
play is less intrinsically theatrical than his situational conceits. Whatever the validity of these discoveries, Albee remains
the most versatile and accomplished playwright of his generation, a master of the spare and cerebral no less than of the
idiomatically fulsome.

Jack Gelber's *The Connection* (1959) was the most famous
production of Julian Beck and Judith Malina's Living Theatre
before tax problems forced the group into European exile. In
this antiillusionist work, four heroin addicts fritter away their
time onstage waiting for "the connection" who will bring their
drug fix. Four jazz musicians mirror them, and the ostensible
director of the piece and two cameramen who are filming it as
a documentary "turn on" with the addicts when the connection

arrives. The traditional distinction between the audience and the actors is collapsed in the mode of Pirandello and Beckett, but more aggressively. Actors beg money for their fixes in the lobby and in the aisles, and they harangue from the stage with quasi-improvised charges that the audience is "hooked" as much as they—on God, on hope, on whatever sustains their lives. Albee's *The Zoo Story* would conceivably have failed off-Broadway had *The Connection* not prepared an audience a year earlier.

The Connection is more rigidly composed than it appears in production, and its mix of rhetoric, theater, and incidental music is both adroit and enlivening, a fine rhythmic counterpoint. The play wreaked havoc on theatrical pieties in 1959 and inspired a host of spin-offs that made a cult of improvisation, but it is historically important for enlarging theatrical sensibilities of the period. Gelber has written other plays— *The Apple* (1961), *Square in the Eye* (1965), *The Cuban Thing* (1968), *Sleep* (1972), and *Jack Gelber's New Play: Rehearsal* (1976)—but none has expanded theatrical awareness to the same degree as *The Connection*.

Arthur Kopit first came to Broadway in 1962 with *Oh Dad, Poor Dad, Mama's Hung You in the Closet and I'm Feelin' So Sad*, a wickedly funny play that spoofed Tennessee Williams's *The Rose Tattoo* (1951), satirized absurdist drama, and exploded psychological clichés about the emasculated American male and his mother. The son and his widowed mother in the play are the Rosepettles; her suitor is Commodore Roseabove; a catalytic seductress is Rosalie; and a pet piranha responds to Rosalinda. "Poor Dad" is kept in the closet in his coffin, except when he tumbles out with expressionist pertinency. "My son shall have the light," Madame Rosepettle intones, majestically echoing Ibsen's Mrs. Alving. And so it goes, a play described by its author as "A Pseudoclassical Tragifarce in a Bastard French Tradition," extravagant, parodic, uninhibitedly camp.

Plays that followed *Oh Dad*—notably *Asylum, or, What the Gentlemen Are Up To, Not to Mention the Ladies* (1963),

The Conquest of Everest (1964), and *The Day the Whores Came Out to Play Tennis* (1965)—continue in the same madcap vein. *Indians* (1969), Kopit's most esteemed work, is weightier but no less a tour de force. Compounding Buffalo Bill Cody's Wild West Show, a federal investigation of Indian grievances in 1886, and other points in time, it launches an attack on America's historical treatment of the Indian and on the mythology by which that treatment has been justified. It uses the camp theatricality of Kopit's earlier work with a seriousness that looks forward to *Wings* (1978), a short play that explores the mind of a stroke victim deprived of the ability to create and understand language. The black humor and camp frivolity of Kopit's early work seem to be evolving into as fine a seriousness. *Indians* and *Wings* are intellectually formidable and deeply felt plays that command the stage with authority.

Murray Schisgal began off-Broadway as an absurdist but gradually discovered on Broadway that he is a farceur. His essential gift is for screwball characters: a postman in *The Tiger* (1963) who aspires to be a sex maniac; an apparent Caucasian who has Chinese parents but plays at being Jewish in *The Chinese* (1970); a young man in *An American Millionaire* (1974) unable to consummate a third marriage because of his ill-timed faints. Too often Schisgal's plays lack any kind of development and simply posit such characters as travesties of psychological and social clichés. But in *Luv* (1964) and *All over Town* (1974), farce rises through absurdism as cream to the top. *Luv* is a deliciously comic play, set entirely on a bridge, in which a man eager to marry his paramour tries to palm off his wife on a suicidal friend. *All over Town* is even more extravagantly farcical, a whirligig of a play in which a moonstruck psychiatrist and his family try to reform a delivery boy they mistake for a Lothario who has put five women and nine children on the welfare rolls. With a large cast of eccentrics and a profusion of exits and entrances, it is a classic Feydeau farce, as impalpable as air, as buoyant as a mote of dust.

Trained as a philosopher, Jack Richardson gave the theater several intellectually adventurous works before pursuing other interests. *The Prodigal* (1960), his first play, re-creates the Orestes myth. With fine lucidity and contemporary relevance, it pits society's need for heroes against the pleasures of individual lack of commitment. *Gallows Humor* (1961) is as philosophically deliberative a work as *The Prodigal* but more original in form—an assemblage of two one-act plays and a prologue. In the first of the two, a condemned man who has never been more than half alive is persuaded by an agent of the state to climb the gallows spiritedly in order to confound opponents of capital punishment; in the second, his executioner struggles to overcome his own dispiritedness with less success. *Lorenzo* (1963) and *Xmas in Las Vegas* (1965) scrutinize equivalent matters of life and death but with less dramaturgical imagination, and they have not been successful on the stage. Their failure must be credited in part to a prevailing distaste in the United States for a theater of ideas.

OFF-OFF-BROADWAY

The lessening difference between Broadway and off-Broadway gave rise during the 1960s to a newly uncommercial alternative, clumsily dubbed "off-off-Broadway" theater, which established itself in New York City lofts, churches, and coffee houses whose names have become synonymous with avant-garde experiment: Caffe Cino, La Mama Experimental Theatre Club, Judson Poets' Theater, and Theatre Genesis, to name only the best known. At the same time, regional theaters began to take on a new vitality and significance, and companies in Louisville, San Francisco, Washington, Dallas, Chicago, Minneapolis, and Los Angeles developed national prominence. Although somewhat less adventurous than off-off-Broadway theaters and therefore less hospitable to new playwrights, these regional theaters have proved more hospitable than Broadway to new talent and have helped make it possible for playwrights and plays to build substantial reputations without the imprimatur of a Broadway production. Indeed, the most often performed play of the 1970s was a play that never attempted Broadway production—Jerome Lawrence and Robert E. Lee's *The Night Thoreau Spent in Jail* (1970).

As it became clear that Broadway was *disengagé*, turned by economics into a purveyor of conventional, pretested goods, the more fluid world of off-off-Broadway proved itself aggressively *engagé*—sensitive to the civil rights struggle, to the sexual revolution, to urban malaise, and to the antiwar movement. Evidencing this sensitivity, off-off-Broadway dramatists waged war on the well-made play that is Broadway's staple, spurning its neatness and logic in favor of the randomness and illogicality that seemed part of the new awareness. Drama cooperatives like the Living Theatre, the Open Theatre, and The Performance Group consciously deemphasized the verbal and the representational elements in their productions in the name of "relevance," "immediacy," "presence." Megan Terry cautioned the director of *Viet Rock* (1966) to treat her visual images as more important than her words. A great deal of theatrical silliness was bred under the aegis of uncommercialism and ideological relevance, of course, but off-off-Broadway also nurtured playwrights such as Sam Shepard (b. 1943), David Mamet (b. 1947), and David Rabe (b. 1940), probably the most important American dramatists of the 1970s.

As the recipient of a Pulitzer Prize and ten Obie awards, Sam Shepard dominates the off-off-Broadway stage. His early works offer little in the way of characterization, plot, and sustained dialogue, but Shepard substitutes a hallucinatory naturalism for these, and assembles bits and pieces of story into configurations with an extraordinary psychological resonance. In early plays such as *La Turista* (1967), *The Unseen Hand* (1969), and *Operation Sidewinder* (1970), he conjures verbal and visual images into surreal visions of the familiar. At the end of *La Turista*, for instance, his protagonist runs full tilt toward the back of the set and crashes through a wall, leaving an outline in the shattered backdrop that haunts memory. In *Operation Sidewinder*, an experimental computer adopts the persona of an ancient Indian snake god, and in a provocative overlay of mythologies, the play ends as government troops surround Indians engaged in its worship. Such configurations suggest that Shepard is more interested in playing on the audience's nerves and subliminal associations than in orchestrating explicable meanings.

Shepard has proved particularly adept at working with configurations of the popular imagination, and his dramatis personae include not only cowboys and Indians, but rock musicians, science-fiction creatures, and cinema celebrities. In *Mad Dog Blues* (1971), Marlene Dietrich, Mae West, Captain Kidd, and Paul Bunyan join in a hunt for buried treasure, and in *The Tooth of Crime* (1973) a rock superstar named Hoss is challenged by a younger musician named Crow in a black-leather reprise of *Gunfight at the O.K. Corral*. Intense, metaphorically powerful, allusively resonant, such plays are a provocative distillation of American mythology.

Shepard's recent work has been preoccupied with the grisliness of family life. *Curse of the Starving Class* (1976), *Buried Child* (1978), and *True West* (1980) are dramas in which family members wound and terrorize one another with an intensity not felt in the theater since *Long Day's Journey into Night*. Although more straightforwardly plotted than their predecessors, these plays have the same mythic resonance and startling *coups de théâtre* that distinguish Shepard's work from the beginning. "Ya think there's room for a real Western these days?" one brother asks another in *True West*, and the play answers his question by striking a final tableau as memorable as the shattered backdrop in *La Turista*—the two brothers squaring off in near darkness, their murderous rage archetypal and irresolvable.

Like Shepard, David Mamet shows a fondness for the staccato rhythm of dramatic bits and pieces. He also shows a fondness for two-part harmony. *Duck Variations* (1972) is a wry sequence of vignettes about two old men who sit on a park bench discussing the habits of ducks and a variety of other subjects, notably mortality. More acerbic in tone, *Sexual Perversity in Chicago* (1974) is a string of vignettes about two couples torn by the machismo code. *A Life in the Theatre* (1977) is Mamet's most elaborate sequence—one in which two actors of different schools and generations joust by reprising virtually every acting style of the century as they work their way through a repertoire of scenes both onstage and backstage. In recent works Mamet tends to abandon sequential elaboration in favor of the isolated vignette, as in *Reunion* (1977), *Dark Pony* (1977), *Mr. Happiness* (1978), and *Shoeshine* (1979). Fragile but carefully wrought moments of drama, these minimalist works eschew the more obvious forms of development in order to nuance a relationship or tableau. *Edmund* (1982) coordinates such scenes into a story about one man's uncontrollable panic.

The Water Engine (1977) is Mamet's most elaborate mosaic of bits and pieces and his finest work to date—a series of short, abrupt scenes superimposing the make-believe world of a radio play upon its foregrounded dramatization in a Chicago studio. Mamet has had his greatest success, however, with *American Buffalo* (1975), a relatively naturalistic work about three men who aspire to steal a coin collection alleged to include a particularly valuable buffalo nickel. In several ways *American Buffalo* is Mamet's version of Pinter's *The Caretaker*: its losers are a threesome who alternately abuse and support one another, and their exchanges draw electrical energy from the meanness of everyday speech.

A veteran of the Vietnam conflict, David Rabe rode the crest of anti-Vietnam sentiment with his first two plays, *Sticks and Bones* (1969) and *The Basic Training of Pavlo Hummel* (1971). The first is an absurdist drama about a young man named David who has been blinded in Vietnam and returns after demobilization to his father Ozzie, his mother Harriet, and his brother Rick—not really the family of the 1950s situation comedy but unfeeling dolts who encourage him to commit suicide. The second is about the brutalization of a young army recruit and his senseless death. Although they carefully avoid the incessant antiwar rhetoric that makes George Tabori's (b. 1914) *Pinkville* (1970) inappreciable and the sort of

sentimentality that makes Ron Cowen's (b. 1944) *Summertree*
(1968) embarrassing, both of Rabe's plays seem today too much
a product of the guilt complexes of their period. Christopher
Durang's (b. 1949) *The Vietnamization of New Jersey* (1977),
a parody of *Sticks and Bones*, successfully exposes the cliché
that informs Rabe's plays—that America's involvement in
Vietnam was a spillover of its domestic violence.

  Streamers (1976), the third play in Rabe's Vietnam trilogy,
is his best work to date. Although set in an army barracks, the
play has almost nothing to say about Vietnam, but a great deal
to say about the exclusivity of groups. Two black and two white
soldiers jockey themselves into groups of three, which dissolve
and reform with balletic grace as the play builds to a bloody
climax. *Streamers* is free of the capricious lyricism and strain-
ing symbolism of its predecessors and is powerfully naturalistic
in its handling of several complex characters. Its success suggests that Rabe's forte is realism.

  Avant-garde experimentation enjoys a continuing mystique in the off-off-Broadway theater, but much of its mystique
is undeserved. With little opportunity for the kind of training
that television and radio drama offer in Western Europe,
American playwrights tend to rely on inborn and instinctive
talent rather than on professionally acquired skills and to substitute energy and commitment for the inadequacy of their ex-
posure to dramatic tradition. Seeming to require little in the
way of professional training, experiment too often becomes vin-
dication—an excuse for unprofessionalism. Nevertheless,
much of the most arresting theater of the past few decades is
avant-garde, and a number of dramatists who work in the experimental off-off-Broadway theater have earned substantial
reputations. Sam Shepard is the most distinguished member
of a constellation that includes Megan Terry (b. 1932), Jean-
Claude Van Itallie (b. 1936), Israel Horovitz (b. 1939), John
Hawkes (b. 1925), Steve Tesich (b. 1936?), Jules Feiffer (b.
1929), John Guare (b. 1938), Terrence McNally (b. 1939), Richard France (b. 1938), Ronald Ribman (b. 1932), María Irene
Fornés (b. 1930), and David Starkweather (b. 1935).

More of an avant-gardist than either Mamet or Rabe, Megan Terry is a devotee of "transformation," an acting exercise in which the actor plays a series of different characters without a formal break or transition between the roles, and which Terry was exposed to during her long association with Joseph Chaikin and his Open Theatre collective. In plays such as *Calm Down Mother* (1965), *Keep Tightly Closed in a Cool Dry Place* (1965), *The Gloaming, Oh My Darling* (1965), and *Comings and Goings* (1966), she elevates transformation technique to a principle of dramatic construction and even to an article of belief—that each human being *is* many individuals. *Calm Down Mother* is staged with three performers who dramatize eight different character relationships in a free-flowing montage; and *The Gloaming, Oh My Darling* brings to the surface varying personae of two old women as their memories wax and wane. Such plays sacrifice motivational coherence for impact, and they tend, perforce, to emphasize presentational values. Consistent with this aesthetic, Terry works out her dramaturgies in ensemble rehearsal as much as on paper. A script, she says, is merely "a trampoline for actors and director."

Terry first attracted attention with *Viet Rock* (1966), a musical play that pretends to glorify popular clichés but actually lampoons the slogans of both pacifism and militarism, targeting above all else the language of insensibility. Her work since *Viet Rock* continues to be dramaturgically inventive and culturally responsive. *Jack-Jack* (1968), *The Tommy Allen Show* (1969), *Babes in the Bighouse* (1974), and *Attempted Rescue on Avenue B* (1979) are noteworthy, but Terry's most impressive work is *Approaching Simone* (1970), a tribute to the philosopher Simone Weil that rings changes on all its characters except Weil, who stands monolithically above the transformational flux.

Like Terry, Jean-Claude Van Itallie was a mainstay of the Open Theatre and maintained professional ties with the group until it disbanded in 1973. While his first works are little more than cabaret sketches, Van Itallie struck a major chord with *America Hurrah* (1966), a series of three short plays that mock

America's machine-honed culture with a dramaturgy of masks, absurdist conundrums, and papier-mâché puppets. Van Itallie's dramaturgy is influenced by the Open Theatre's esteem for the transformation sequence, but also by myth and totemistic ritual. In *The Serpent: A Ceremony* (1969), his most estimable success, the Genesis story provides the framework for a mythic understanding of human behavior. Our prototypical forebears are transformed into such figures as John F. Kennedy and Martin Luther King and discover modes of begetting and bloodletting with an enthusiasm that resonates down the ages. Although his plays tend to be more visual than aural, Van Itallie is a thoughtful writer who insists that actors adhere to his words, even though he regards words as the tip of the dramatic iceberg.

Like Terry and Van Itallie, Israel Horovitz has very nearly made a career of the short play. He rose to prominence with a double bill composed of *The Indian Wants the Bronx* and *It's Called the Sugar Plum* in 1968, playlets that invoke both comedy and terror in carefully dissimilar ways. In the first, two New York toughs harass an East Indian whom they come upon at a bus stop, and the victim's inability to understand their English makes the escalating violence of their harassment a grim and terrible joke. The second is a mock love story that begins with violence and high feeling and shifts to romantic banalities with no less frightening effect. Horovitz's numerous sketches tend to be works of this kind, naturalistic renderings of absurdist situations. At their worst they are one-note jokes swollen into mummery, but at their best they are crystalline turns of metaphor that rival Ionesco's one-act plays.

Horovitz's most substantial achievement is a sequence of seven short works, not yet performed in series, which he calls *The Wakefield Plays* (1979) and subdivides into *The Alfred Trilogy* and *The Quannapowitt Quartet* (1976). The three Alfred plays deal with Alfred Webber, a man of little charm and less memory, who returns to his hometown to explore old crimes against his family only to discover that the crimes were all his own. The plays of *The Quannapowitt Quartet* are unrelated except in their theme of loneliness. *Stage Directions* (1976) is the most dramaturgically interesting work of the quartet—a staging of a funeral at which the grown children of the deceased have no dialogue except a compendium of stage directions, which they use as dialogue to describe their formalized grief.

Although known primarily for his fiction, John Hawkes produced a series of four avant-garde plays during the 1960s: *The Questions* (1966), *The Wax Museum* (1966), *The Undertaker* (1967), and *The Innocent Party* (1968). As much as his novels, Hawkes's plays seem an effluvium of the subconscious, a haunting dream of overripe innocence and insidiously accommodating brutishness. This effect is due in part to Hawkes's chill detachment from conventional morality, in part to an absorbing dialogue so unconvincing as conversation that it seems to locate itself in a mental world independent of the characters' physical circumstances. *The Questions* is set appositely in "a white setting so neutral and shadowed that it might be a courtroom, doctor's office, sun parlor, or the pure space of psychic activity." Hawkes's plays are interesting as experiments because they test how far conversational narrative can displace dramatic action, but their final effect is too dramaturgically lean to satisfy the eye. With slight modification, they would make admirable radio plays.

Yugoslav-born Steve Tesich has an engaging view of American life that best expresses itself in a blend of absurdism and domestic farce, most notably in *Baba Goya* (1973) and *Division Street* (1980). The first is a madcap comedy about a household in Queens made up of strange, almost unrelated relations bound together by an elemental need for relationship. The second is as charming a comedy about a 1960s radical who tries a decade later to shed his past and adopt a fashionable self-interest, only to find himself hounded by a black policeman, a murderous Serbian, and an activist associate. *The Carpenters* (1970), *Lake of the Woods* (1971), *Passing Game* (1977), and a trilogy of short plays entitled *Touching Bottom* (1979) are more purely absurdist drama—increasingly assured in

their technique and not without interest, but without the com-
ical effervescence of *Baba Goya*. Tesich has recently enjoyed
success as a Hollywood screenwriter.

Jules Feiffer brings his fine skills as a cartoonist to several
revues based on his comic strips, notably to *Feiffer's People*
(1968) and *Hold Me!* (1977). He has also written several full-
length plays. *Little Murders* (1967) is a cartoonish tribute to
the urban mythology of muggings, obscene phone calls, and
power failures; *The White House Murder Case* (1970) a tribute
to intemperateness in the presidential cabinet. More tonally
consistent than these, *Knock Knock* (1976) is Feiffer's best play.
It centers on an ideological battle between two vaudevillians,
Cohen and Abe, and Joan of Arc, who tries to gather them into
Noah's Ark in a glorious confusion of homophones. Less polit-
ically satiric than its predecessors and more verbally playful,
Knock Knock is spun-sugar philosophizing—a comedic exam-
ination of faith and commitment, of immersion in and with-
drawal from the world.

John Guare brings an anarchic energy to the theater, almost an inspired madness. Half clown and half black humorist,
he delights in subjects like murder and religious mania, and
he has a gift for spinning fantasies—about selling the rights
to one's suicide, for instance, and about leaves that bud blue
in the spring. Parents are his obsessional subject. In *The House
of Blue Leaves* (1971), *Rich and Famous* (1976), *Landscape of
the Body* (1977), and *Bosoms and Neglect* (1979), parents are
variously shot, riddled with cancer, even accused of murdering
their sons, but somehow they never understand the point of
this melodramatic farce or admit their insufficiency. In two
plays that seem part of a gathering trilogy, *Gardenia* (1982)
and *Lydie Breeze* (1982), Guare attempts to come to terms with
his Furies. As much as their predecessors, these are stories of
undying family battles, of parents unfaithful to themselves and
to their children, of murder, suicide, and revenge. But without
renouncing humor altogether, Guare largely abandons his cartoonish manner and displaces the outré glitter of his earlier
dramaturgy with a more sober chiaroscuro. At once lyrical,

elegiac, and melodramatic, *Gardenia* and *Lydie Breeze* are that most unexpected of developments in Guare's oeuvre—melodramas that edge toward tragedy rather than toward farce.

Terrence McNally brings a more political sensibility to a humor as giddily black as Guare's, addressing himself to the military draft in *Next* (1968), to presidential assassination in *Witness* (1968), and to the Vietnam involvement in a series of plays. *Where Has Tommy Flowers Gone?* (1971) is his most accomplished black comedy, a sweetly macabre play about a young man who blows up New York City's Lincoln Center theater complex in a spirit of 1960s prankishness. It is McNally's sociopolitical conceit that violence, murder, and presidential assassination have become the grotesquerie of a Charles Addams cartoon, a camp weirdness instead of tragedy. As the taste for black comedy has faded, he has turned to more straightforward farce, first in a critical disaster entitled *Whiskey* (1973), then in *The Ritz* (1975), a successful Broadway play in which Mafiosi run amok in a gay bathhouse.

Richard France has written plays in a variety of experimental modes that are individually interesting, if not commercially successful. *Envoys* (1965), for instance, is a verse drama that delicately orchestrates 105 haiku, and *A Day in the Life* (1973) is an absorbing mix of realism and surrealism, complete with mannequins and the projected shadow of an outsize rat. In *One Day in the Life of Ivan Denisovich* (1975), an adaptation of Alexander Solzhenitsyn's novel, the title character is entirely silent—with elegiac effect. France's most successful play is *Station J* (1979), an epic drama about the incarceration of Japanese-Americans in West Coast prison camps during World War II. Scenes that depict the upheaval in the life of a single Nisei family alternate with a short Noh play, with scenes of angry mobs and political demagogues, with a Fireside Chat, and with the Supreme Court decision that allowed the prison camps to exist. In assembling this shameful history, France gives it mythic sweep and tragic stature, a combination that interracial themes seem to evoke in American drama.

Ronald Ribman has received less critical attention than he merits. This is partly because his work is too various to assert itself as an oeuvre: *Harry, Noon and Night* (1965) is a wickedly perverse comedy about an intemperate homosexual; *The Journey of the Fifth Horse* (1966) is an adaptation of Turgenev's *The Diary of a Superfluous Man*; and *Fingernails Blue as Flowers* (1971) is an absurdist fantasy about a paranoid ensconced on a Jamaican beach. *The Ceremony of Innocence* (1967) is set in eleventh-century England, *The Poison Tree* (1976) in a California prison, and *Cold Storage* (1977) in a cancer hospital. All, however, are dramas of character, of tormented souls at loggerheads with their circumstances.

Ribman's critics argue rightly that he has a deficient sense of dramatic structure. The parallel is too rigidly worked in *The Journey of the Fifth Horse* between the landowner, Chulkaturin, and Zoditch, a publisher's reader who scoffs at Chulkaturin's diary; and the symbiotic emotional therapy in *Cold Storage* is too pat, a garrulous patient named Parmigian dovetailing too well with a repressed patient named Landau. But Ribman's tone is thickly textured, layered with both humor and sadness, a substantial pleasure altogether. He remains a playwright without a major play, but with considerable promise.

María Irene Fornés is another little-known playwright, but unlike Ribman she has a sense of dramatic structure markedly her own. Her early plays, *There! You Died* (1963), *The Successful Life of 3* (1965), and *Promenade* (1965), are highly stylized absurdist works that survey the role of power in human relationships. In *A Vietnamese Wedding* (1967) and the highly esteemed *Fefu and Her Friends* (1977), Fornés abandons absurdism in favor of paratheatrical "happenings," the goal of which is not so much entertainment as an alteration of consciousness. In the first, four actors play host to ten persons from the audience who participate in the Vietnamese nuptials, and they play host finally to the entire audience in a postwedding celebration. In the second, the audience is divided into four groups and invited into the eponymous Fefu's home, where she and her women friends go about various activities that illumine the pleasures of female friendship. A feminist understanding of sexual anamorphosis is the play's goal. *Dr. Kheal* (1968) is more orthodox theater, a one-man play in which the audience is alternately harangued and cajoled by a classroom instructor as entirely mad as he is brilliant. Born in Cuba, Fornés has recently been active in the New York City native-Spanish theater with plays such as *Cap-a-Pie* (1975), *Lolita in the Garden* (1977), and *Eyes on the Harem* (1979).

If Fornés's contributions to the theater are little known, David Starkweather's contributions are virtually ignored. Yet Starkweather represents experimental theater at its eclectic best. He borrows techniques freely from dance, mime, and musical theater to stylize his unrealistic plays, and he has a finely tuned sense of how to make such diverse borrowings interact dramaturgically. In *You May Go Home Again* (1963), the story of an executioner who goes home emotionally as well as physically for his sister's wedding, Starkweather uses choreographic effects to shape and stylize the movements of his actors, music to counterpoint and emphasize his dramatic action, and fantastical costuming to underscore his stylized artificiality. "A domestic Noh in one-act," he calls the play, but its workings are so theatrically elemental that they evoke medieval English drama as well as the Japanese theater.

The dramaturgical blend is Starkweather's hallmark. In *The Poet's Papers* (1971) he even blends absurdism and the Renaissance masque. His conceit in the play is that the Poet has died and that the President and his Secretaries of Logic, Reality, and the Ulterior must devise a suitable memorial. Congress becomes an orchestra, the Poet performs as an exotic dancer, and the President and his advisors transform variously into the King and Queen of the Anals, sometimes the Orals. The procession of scenes grows increasingly frenetic, but with consummate theatricality Starkweather anchors the chaos with a metronomic ticking that grows louder and more insistent in the last section of the play, as if one's heartbeat were aggrieved. He is a master of such expressionistic effects.

Although avant-gardism sets the tone of the off-off-Broadway theater, a significant number of its playwrights cast their lot with realism to write dramas about middle-class Americans who live their lives in living rooms. Heirs of Ibsen and Chekhov rather than of Ionesco and Pirandello, these dramatists are preeminently orchestrators of mood. Lanford Wilson (b. 1937), Mark Medoff (b. 1940), Thomas Babe (b. 1941), Michael Weller (b. 1942), Preston Jones (1936–1979), Dick Goldberg (b. 1947), Howard Sackler (1929–1982), John Ford Noonan (b. 1943), Albert Innurato (b. 1949), William Hanley (b. 1931), Robert Patrick (b. 1937), and Mart Crowley (b. 1935) are important among them. Two actors, Michael Cristofer (b. 1946) and Jason Miller (b. 1939), also show talent as realistic playwrights.

Lanford Wilson's plays are a series of portraits as richly textured as they are realistic. *The Madness of Lady Bright* (1964) is half grit and half whipped cream, a tour de force about a homosexual transvestite who fears he is losing his looks. *Balm in Gilead* (1965) is a group portrait of upper-Broadway lowlifes; *The Rimers of Eldritch* (1966), of lives touched by murder in a small Midwestern town. Wilson also cultivates the heightened realism of Brecht's "alienation effect." His characters address long monologues directly to the audience and say things like "I get to begin the play now." Their stories tend to emerge in fragments rather than in sequential plots, often in overlapping or simultaneous dialogues that interlock rhythmically better than they do conceptually. Wilson's genius is not for the well-made play, but for the realistic ensemble piece in which each character and patch of dialogue makes a distinct claim of its own.

Wilson's most recent works have enjoyed wide popularity, especially *The Hot l Baltimore* (1973), *5th of July* (1978), and *Talley's Folly* (1979). *The Hot l Baltimore* is set in a decaying residential hotel peopled with whores, hustlers, and septuagenarians, and its *Grand Hotel* formula is so entirely successful that it inspired a (short-lived) television series. Installments in a projected sequence of five plays about an extended Missouri family, *5th of July* and *Talley's Folly* are unabashedly sentimental. Wilson's stylistic panache makes such plays more than commercial trifles, but his drift toward commercial Broadway fare is unmistakable.

Mark Medoff's plays are unrealistic in their premises but elaborately realistic in detail. His typical protagonist is a male who brutally compels others to face truths about themselves and their situations, not in the abstract service of truth, but as an act of psychopathic aggression, both sexual and intellectual. *When You Comin Back, Red Ryder?* (1973) is his best play—the story of four people savagely manipulated by a stray gunman who forces them to realize they have evaded emotional honesty. As in his earlier plays *The Kramer* (1972) and *The Wager* (1973), Medoff suggests that his characters are better for the truth-teller's brutality, however unlikely it may be that a gunman should concern himself with their delusions. In *Children of a Lesser God* (1979), Medoff offers the negative side of this unsentimental logic and writes a play about a marriage disintegrating for lack of such a truth-teller. His main character is a deaf woman who refuses to learn to speak or read lips.

Because his plays tend to formulism and even to cliché, the gifted Thomas Babe gives the impression that he has not yet found his subject. Southern women are compelled to quarter General Sherman in *Rebel Women* (1976), a tale somewhat more than twice told. The emotional link between sadistic policemen and their prisoners is wrought as if for the first time in *A Prayer for My Daughter* (1977), and the Wild West revisionism spawned by America's bicentenary is played *da capo* in *Fathers and Sons* (1978). Babe's plays lack thematic focus as well as originality in plotting. *Taken in Marriage* (1979) is a comedy of manners that puns eloquently on its title, but nothing more to the point evolves when four New York City women find themselves the only attendants at a wedding rehearsal in rural New Hampshire. *Salt Lake City Skyline* (1979), a play about the 1915 trial of Joe Hill, wavers between the hagiographical and the hardheaded. The appeal of Babe's plays is their subtle alternation of speech and silence, and their fluid rhythms of revelation and concealment—achievements of manner rather than of substance.

Michael Weller has clearly found his subject in the 1960s decade, and in plays such as *Loose Ends* (1979) and *Split* (1980), he seems caught up in a love-hate relationship with the decade's more exaggerated sentiments. *Moonchildren* (1971), his most successful play, is a memorial of sorts to those 1960s American youths who thought of themselves as "laid back." A funny, often touching play, it deals plotlessly with eight students who share a ramshackle apartment and evade both responsibility and the risks of genuine feeling with relentlessly witty "put-ons" that strip social and emotional realities of their significance. Weller's subsequent work has matched neither the brightness of *Moonchildren*'s wit nor the delicate balance of its understanding.

As a resident playwright of the Dallas Theater Center, Preston Jones was uncomfortable with the concept of regional theater, but his rise to national fame was an important milestone for such theaters—the first instance in which an American playwright earned a major reputation without the benefit of a New York imprimatur. He is best known for *A Texas Trilogy*, three full-length plays set in a small town in Texas named Bradleyville. *The Last Meeting of the Knights of the White Magnolia* (1973), *Lu Ann Hampton Laverty Oberlander* (1974), and *The Oldest Living Graduate* (1974) are thinly plotted and modest in presentation, but they offer well-rounded characters and an almost palpable sense of place. Their appeal is to a certain extent preservational. The main characters in all three plays subsist on idealized memories of the past, and their politics, social attitudes, and language are so regionally suggestive that they seem exhibits in a folk museum, the stuff of life once removed from reality.

Thus far in his career, Dick Goldberg is also a preservationalist, a devotee of the well-made play and a chronicler of traditional Jewish family life. He spread his wings by founding the American-Jewish Theatre in Massachusetts, then wrote *Black Zion* (1971), a play all struts and braces, in which a black maid takes a Jewish family hostage in her sympathy with television reports of escalating racial violence in the ghettos. With *Family Business* (1978), Goldberg's dramaturgy took uncertain but more successful flight. A realistic melodrama, it portrays four Jewish sons who attack each other with love and hatred in a dispute over the division of their millionaire father's estate. The plot is leaden, and Goldberg manipulates his characters with a heavy hand, but the characterization is winged, and the sibling conflict has a fine authenticity.

As an experienced director of Elizabethan drama, Howard Sackler brought to his play writing a feel for historical subjects and a taste for Shakespearean abundance and sweep. These things are most evident in *The Great White Hope* (1967), a work that traces the career of the black prizefighter Jack Johnson from his victory over the white champion in 1908, through a trumped-up arrest and European exile, to his loss of the world heavyweight title in 1915. A chronicle of race no less than a drama of personal relationships, the play is a staggering array of nineteen scenes that arch from success to failure with tragic inevitability. Among Sackler's other works, only *Semmelweiss* (1977) has the epic sweep of *The Great White Hope*, but Sackler was equally impressive as a playwright of mood and atmosphere—notably in *Sarah* (1965), a sepulchral inquest drama set on the bare stage of a mid-Victorian ballet theater, and in *The Pastime of Monsieur Robert* (1969), a play about de Sadean fantasies set loose in an eighteenth-century French chateau.

John Ford Noonan is a deft jokesmith with a compassion for those who suffer from sexual incapacity and repression. *Older People* (1972) is a series of thirteen vignettes about the geriatric set bidding adieu to the carnal itch. If slightly sentimentalized and generally predictable, they mesh with the graceful cross-referencing of a fugue: a homosexual couple troubled by impotence echoes a heterosexual couple with the same problem; characters are transformed into other characters like shifting tonalities; and a suitcase relinquished in one vignette is picked up in the next like a lost chord. In *A Coupla White Chicks Sitting Around Talking* (1980), sex is once again the insouciant subject as a Texas slattern teaches a repressed Westchester matron about carnal abandon. There is no depth in Noonan's plays and little insight, but his lightness of touch is itself an art.

Albert Innurato has a larger dramatic voice than Noonan, indeed a taste for extravagance. The central character in *The Transfiguration of Benno Blimpie* (1977) is an adolescent boy who weighs five hundred pounds and sits marmoreally in the center of the stage, aching for love and approval, fending off insults with self-mocking wit. *Gemini* (1977), Innurato's most successful play, has a whole cast of misfits and hysterics, and the author embroils them in every kind of excess: a crisis of sexual identity, several brawls, an attempted suicide, a grandly comic birthday celebration, boisterous idiosyncrasies, blanketing good will, and a happy ending. Innurato's extravagance is less successful in *Ulysses in Traction* (1977), a play about drama students and their teachers in the middle of a ghetto riot, because he does not adequately develop his characters as persons. Without fully rounded and appealing characters, his extravagance lacks an essential heartbeat.

William Hanley has written several interesting plays as well as novels and screenplays, but he is best known for *Slow Dance on the Killing Ground* (1962), a play set in a Brooklyn luncheonette and peopled by a schizophrenic black man, a white girl in search of an abortionist, and a German counterman who abandoned his Jewish wife and child to the Nazis. The play moves from naturalism to surrealism when the two interlopers put the counterman on mock trial for their collective sins. Hanley has not surpassed the imaginative vigor and tenderness of *Slow Dance on the Killing Ground*, but *Mrs. Dally Has a Lover* (1962) is a worthy one-acter.

Robert Patrick has been widely produced off-off-Broadway but is known almost entirely for his best play, *Kennedy's Children* (1973). In a circuitous route to success, the play had its premiere off-off-Broadway, moved to a failing pub-theater in London, then to the West End, and finally, in 1975, to Broadway. An elegy for the 1960s and an offspring of *Slow Dance on the Killing Ground, Kennedy's Children* is made up of discontinuous monologues by five of the decade's fallouts as they sit in a bar on New York City's Lower East Side. A Kennedy cultist, a Vietnam veteran, a homosexual actor, a bruised flower child, a faded blond who had hoped to succeed Marilyn Monroe as the country's goddess—each is an emblematic survivor of a shipwrecked state; each, an island of disillusionment. Bittersweet nostalgia and occasional self-pity haunt their tales of wasted dreams, but the playwright's wit cuts through undue sentiment, and his idiomatic richness imparts an edge to barstool rhetoric. A generation's truth rings in *Kennedy's Children*, and its resonance is great.

Mart Crowley's *The Boys in the Band* (1968) is as much a milestone in theatrical consciousness as Hansberry's *A Raisin in the Sun*. A story of seven homosexual men celebrating the birthday of one of their number, it is the first important play in the American theater to portray homosexuals without condescension or censure. Self-pity is another matter: "You show me a happy homosexual, and I'll show you a gay corpse," murmurs an autobiographical character. That same character recurs in *Remote Asylum* (1970) and *A Breeze from the Gulf* (1973), but Crowley does not recapture in either of those plays the dialogical bite and ensemble integrity of *The Boys in the Band*. Although gay drama is now an off-off-Broadway fixture, plays like Doric Wilson's (b. 1939) *The West Street Gang* (1977) and Robert Patrick's *T-Shirts* (1978) fall short of Crowley's play as theater. The best gay drama since *The Boys in the Band* includes William M. Hoffman's (b. 1939) and Anthony Holland's (b. 1933) *Cornbury: The Queen's Governor* (1976), an uproariously funny play about Viscount Edward Hyde Cornbury, the transvestite governor of New York and New Jersey in the years 1702–1708; includes also Harvey Fierstein's (b. 1954) *Torch Song Trilogy* (1981), a bittersweet, often touching portrait of a drag queen who takes his keynote from the 1920s ballads that give Fierstein's sequence of plays its title and tone.

Michael Cristofer is primarily an actor, but he has written at least eight plays, one of which, *The Shadow Box* (1975), was a modest Broadway hit in 1977 and was awarded the Pulitzer Prize. *Shadow Box* is the story of three cancer victims living out their lives in an improbable hospice where persons terminally ill are medically undisturbed except by a psychiatrist who monitors their emotions. Because each patient lives in a separate cottage and has no contact with his neighbors, *The Shadow Box* is really three interwoven stories, all relentlessly life affirming, all cagily sparing of medical detail. Sentimentality, not probability, is Cristofer's gift.

Jason Miller is also an actor with demonstrated talent as a playwright. His short plays *Circus Lady* (1967) and *Lou Gehrig Did Not Die of Cancer* (1967) offer some interest, but his stature as a dramatist rests with *That Championship Season* (1972), a study of four high-school athletes who are brought together twenty years after their graduation at a yearly reunion with their coach. The win-at-all-costs philosophy they absorbed as athletes is a moral cancer that has eaten deeply into their lives, setting them at odds with one another; and when their coach is able to forge camaraderie among them once again, it is a chilling indictment of team spirit. First staged in Joseph Papp's Public Theatre, *That Championship Season* moved after six months to Broadway—an instance of Broadway's continuing esteem for the well-made play and of the downward drift of that esteem into the off- and off-off-Broadway theaters.

BLACK THEATER

In the same way that the social unrest of the 1930s gave birth to the proletarian theater, the civil rights struggle that began with the bus boycotts of 1956 and the sit-ins of 1960 gave birth to a socially committed black theater. The great majority of black dramatists write for an ethnically diverse audience and use the traditional forms of naturalism, melodrama, and farce to convey their racial concerns. Notable among these are Alice Childress (b. 1920), James Baldwin (b. 1924), Douglas Turner

Ward (b. 1930), Lonne Elder III (b. 1931), Joseph A. Walker (b. 1935), Charles Fuller (b. 1939), Phillip Hayes Dean (b. 1933?), and the actors Charles Gordone (b. 1925) and Ossie Davis (b. 1917). Ntozake Shange (b. 1948) and Adrienne Kennedy (b. 1931) employ more original, more psychologically expressive dramaturgy. Separatists such as Amiri Baraka (b. 1934) and Ed Bullins (b. 1935), relatively few in number, advocate black theater for a black audience.

Alice Childress is the reigning grande dame of black dramatists, not only because *Gold through the Trees* (1952) was one of the first plays by a black woman to be professionally staged in America, but because she has given a great lady's support to younger black dramatists and started many of them on their way. Deeply committed to social justice, she writes sentimental plays in which victimized blacks speak up for themselves with spirit and courage. *Trouble in Mind* (1955) is about a play rehearsal during which a black actress rebels at unconscious stereotyping by a self-consciously liberal director; *Wine in the Wilderness* (1969) is about black workers who defend their achievements against patronizing black intellectuals. Skirting melodrama, Childress renders her bigoted characters not as witless but as insecure and deluded, unaware of their failings. She consciously spurns the myth of black matriarchy but proffers a vision of black women who refuse to be less strong than the world demands.

Although better known as an essayist and novelist, James Baldwin is the author of two plays. Influenced by his experiences as a child-preacher, he traces in *The Amen Corner* (1965) a black churchwoman's path from a theology of hellfire to a theology of love and sufferance. Influenced by the murder in 1963 of the civil rights worker Medgar Evers, Baldwin depicts in *Blues for Mr. Charlie* (1964) a Southern town before and after a young black man is shot to death by a white shop-owner. Both plays fail badly as theater because they are complicated with too many subplots and overburdened with monologic tirades. Ambivalent about the coalition of whites and middle-class blacks, ambivalent even about the choice between violence and nonviolence, *Blues for Mr. Charlie* fails also as rhetoric. Baldwin is an important influence in the new black theater because he throws the weight of his prestige against the simplifications of agitprop, but he clearly has small instinct for dramatic form.

The plays of Douglas Turner Ward tend to make the point that blacks possessed survival skills long before the advent of radical protest. *Happy Ending* (1965) is a farce in which an "enlightened" black woman is given a lesson in realpolitik by her aunts, who work as domestics and artfully exploit their employers. *Day of Absence* (1965) is similar in tone—a farce about a Southern town paralyzed when all its black citizens disappear one day, bringing essential services to a thudding stop. Gradually, Ward's plays become darker in vision, more acerbic in tone. *The Reckoning* (1969) stages an acrimonious battle of wits between a Southern governor and his blackmailing black mistress, and *Brotherhood* (1970) is an unfunny farce about neighboring black and white families who go through the motions of integrationist brotherhood. Ward built a substantial reputation as an actor before emerging as a playwright and is best known today as the founding genius and artistic director of the Negro Ensemble Company in New York City, a prestigious troupe. The coalition of his various stage skills has advanced black theater immeasurably.

Lonne Elder III came under Ward's influence as a member of the Harlem Writers Guild and assisted him in establishing the Negro Ensemble Company (NEC). Like Ward, he is more interested in rendering the texture of black life than in civil rights polemic. In *Ceremonies in Dark Old Men* (1969), his one major play, he imparts a naturalistic view of the social and psychological stratagems some blacks must practice to keep their self-respect. Set in a barbershop in Harlem, the play is a richly detailed account of one family's tragedy, but contrived and shapeless, a transcript of life more than art. Elder seems now to have abandoned playwriting for screenwriting.

Joseph A. Walker is also affiliated with the Negro Ensemble Company, although several of his plays are more militant fare than is usually produced by the NEC, notably *The Har-rangues* (1969) and *Ododo* (1970). *The River Niger* (1972) is his best play. Dedicated in part "to highly underrated Black dad-dies everywhere," it is a generational play about a father who is shattered by his inability to provide for his family, a son to whom he passes his thwarted dreams, an octogenarian grand-mother who tolerates no dreams at all, and a wife dying of cancer who supports her husband's flight from reality. Like *Ceremonies in Dark Old Men*, the play is so anchored in the black experience that its shapelessness seems Art's concession to Truth. Its melodrama is perhaps Truth's concession to Feel-ing.

Charles Fuller brings historical resonance to plays about black America's struggle for social justice. Both *The Brownsville Raid* (1976) and *A Soldier's Play* (1981) achieve added intensity from their semidocumentary style. The first is a rendering of the 1906 incident in which all the enlisted men in a regiment of black soldiers were discharged, without trial or hearing, for allegedly shooting up the town of Brownsville, Texas. The sec-ond is a courtroom drama, basically a whodunit, about the mur-der of a psychotic black army sergeant during World War II. No simplifier, Fuller treats the historical facts in *The Browns-ville Raid* as ambiguously as they have come down to us in history. Avoiding a simple confrontation between forces of good and evil, he causes his black soldiers to worry whether one of them is indeed guilty of the shoot-up and whether he should be identified. *A Soldier's Play* is an investigation not only of a murder, but of the psychopathology of racial hatred. Fuller is in many ways an angry playwright, but he knows how to harness his anger in the service of theater.

Like Fuller, Phillip Hayes Dean touches black history with a talented finger. In *The Sty of the Blind Pig* (1971), he etches a portrait of black life at the dawn of the civil rights movement and emphasizes the studied gentility of "nice" blacks in the mid-1950s, their mistrust of the spreading bus boycotts, their meek acceptance of the status quo. Through the person of a blind street-singer, Dean insinuates both the past and the future into their atemporal lives. The singer symbolizes the historical condition of being black in white America, a condition that must be proclaimed, sung in the streets. The street-singer will destroy them all, the 1950s blacks are certain, and they turn away from him in the play with a finality that history belies. History might also belie the title portrait in Dean's *Paul Robeson* (1978), for Dean's portrayal of Robeson simplifies some of the facts of the black actor's life and softens some of his extremist positions. It is unlikely, however, that history will judge the play as harshly as James Baldwin and some others who have denounced it as a "pernicious perversion" of Robeson's legacy.

The first black playwright to win the Pulitzer Prize, Charles Gordone stands adamantly opposed to a racially oriented theater. His purpose, he says, is to deal with "the humanity of all people, the love of all people, the will to survive and the will to live—of all people—and the strength of people against fantastic odds." *No Place to Be Somebody* (1969) achieves his purpose on a grand scale. Set in a Greenwich Village bar patronized by both blacks and whites, it is an ensemble play with a wealth of subplots, a range of moods, and sudden bursts of anger, violence, and humor. Hoodlums collide, hookers pine, a disgruntled barkeep takes on the Mafia, and a light-skinned black struggles to establish a racial identity. *Gordone Is a Muthah* (1970) and *The Last Chord* (1976) also reflect Gordone's expansive approach to the stage, but their loose abundance does not equal the richness of *No Place to Be Somebody*.

Ossie Davis is not only a distinguished actor but the author of *Purlie Victorious* (1961), a folk comedy lampooning the Old South that served to ease the black experience onto Broadway. The story of an itinerant black preacher who tries to establish an interracial church in a south Georgia community, it is an amiable frolic through race consciousness, complete with an evil Old Massa, his liberalized son, a witty Uncle Tom, and a kitchen wench who pretends to be her educated aunt in order to claim a racially sidetracked inheritance. Davis's comedy is infectious and quotable: "What's wrong with running?" asks the Uncle Tom figure. "It emancipated more people than Abraham Lincoln ever did!" A militant sermon at the end of the play is an unaccountable addendum to such comic poise.

A veteran of the San Francisco poetry bars, Ntozake Shange came to critical attention with *For Colored Girls Who Have Considered Suicide/When the Rainbow Is Enuf* (1976), an amalgam of texts and dance she calls a "choreopoem." A year later she collaborated with two other women poets and a five-piece jazz band in an entertainment entitled *Where the Mississippi Meets the Amazon* (1977). The texts she has contributed to these works give ardent expression to the experience of being a black woman, especially to the experience of growing up an intelligent and sensitive black woman in a man's world. Yet Shange's texts succeed neither as drama nor as poetry. Too haphazardly structured to have force as drama and too stylistically unrefined to be good poetry, they have the power of undramatic verse sensitively staged, of rude theatrics poetically voiced—a presentational power, in other words, rather than a textual power.

Adrienne Kennedy has occasionally demonstrated a flair for naturalism, but her best work is expressionistically psychological. In *Funnyhouse of a Negro* (1964), she explores the psyche of a young girl, half black and half white, who is visited in the last minutes of her life by mocking specters of her mother, Queen Victoria, the Duchess of Habsburg, Patrice Lumumba, and Jesus Christ. All are projections of the girl's fears and self-loathing; all are unmoored aspects of her tortured consciousness. In the similar dramaturgy of *The Owl Answers* (1966), Anne Boleyn, Geoffrey Chaucer, William the Conqueror, and William Shakespeare pile out of the Tower of London and into a New York City subway car occupied by another half-caste girl. The characters are multipersonal, masked. The girl's mother emerges from Anne Boleyn's papier-mâché body like a locust abandoning its husk. The girl is listed in the dramatis personae as "She who is Clara Passmore who is the Virgin Mary who is the Bastard who is the Owl." Anyone can be anyone in Kennedy's surreal psychology, and her culturally dispossessed heroines are apparently everyone. *A Beast's Story* (1969) practices the same mode of psychological expressionism, blurring, dividing, and combining characters in a black girl's fantasia of unbridled sexual alarm. Kennedy brings a poetic and allusive sensibility to her visions of half-caste conscious- ness, an inexplicable cogency to her bizarre configurations. Few black dramatists are her equal.

Amiri Baraka (formerly LeRoi Jones) has been a major spokesman for black anger since the 1960s. Conceiving of the theater as a revolutionary tool, he blasphemes Christianity, encourages blacks to adopt a separatist stance, and latterly endorses communism. *Dutchman* (1964) is his best and most influential play. Set on a subway train he describes as "the flying underbelly of the city," it is a ritualistic work in which a white slut taunts a middle-class black man for refusing to admit his sociopolitical rage. Despite her intense provocations, the black man does not murder or rape her, as we are led to expect; rather, the white provocateur stabs him and has his dead body thrown from the train. Then she approaches another black man to begin the murderous cycle again. The vitality of the characters is so extraordinary that the exaggerations of the play seem almost justified. Baraka's subsequent plays col- lapse under the burden of similar exaggerations. *A Black Mass* (1966), *Slave Ship* (1967), *S-1* (1976) and *The Motion of History* (1977) are important as indices of black consciousness, impor- tant perhaps as advocacy, but negligible as theater.

Like Baraka, Ed Bullins rode the crest of the 1960s fashion for black awareness in the arts, and he is today the most prolific of contemporary black American playwrights with approxi- mately forty stage works to his credit. "I was a conscious artist before I was a conscious artist-revolutionary," he says, " which has been my salvation and disguise." His plays are straight- forward object lessons about blacks trying to understand them- selves in the context of white society. They are too straight- forward, as a rule, for any but a partisan audience. In *The Gentleman Caller* (1969), a young black male calls on rich, white Mrs. Mann, whose living room is adorned with the mounted heads of a black man, an American Indian, a Chinese, and a Vietnamese. He is saved from Mrs. Mann when a black maid reveals herself as "Queen Mother," cuts Mrs. Mann's throat, and issues a call to black people everywhere to unite behind a bloody sword. Even at his best, as in *Clara's Ole Man* (1968) and *The Taking of Miss Janie* (1975), Bullins is prone to such crudely forceful theatrics. Scenes of wine drinking and drug snorting are his standard occasions for the liberation of truth; rape scenes serve for an enforced recognition of blackness.

American drama is so evanescent a phenomenon and so influenced by economic and social circumstances that its history is difficult to separate from the history of commercially successful productions. Works of interesting writers like Paul Foster (b. 1931), Julie Bovasso (b. 1930), and Wilford Leach (b. 1934) have flickered for a night or two in coffee houses and exist now only in memory, while lesser works have survived through better financing or some quirk of box office appeal. In such a theater, genius is rarely a shaping factor. Indeed, the history of American drama since 1945 is shaped less by intellectual cross-pollination and orderly growth than by a series of reactions against the well-made play, whose nineteenth-century lucidity serves as a focus for all kinds of ideological discontent. It is the stagnation of the American stage that such reactions affect the surface but not the substance of the well-made play. In the tradition that runs from O'Neill's *Long Day's Journey into Night* through Albee's *Who's Afraid of Virginia Woolf?* to Shepard's *Buried Child*, postwar drama continues to play out the moral and generational obsessions of the well-made play, turning the stage into a kind of domestic courtroom complete with investigations, arraignments, and judgments. Probably because they are less vulnerable to popular response, American fiction and poetry have both struck more aesthetically interesting courses than drama, and with results more stimulating to the creative imagination.

4 · POETRY

American poetry written since World War II is extraordinarily various. Schools, movements, and ideologies have not only proliferated but fragmented in the last few decades, with a restlessness born of a nagging dissatisfaction with the reigning modes of verse and a nomadic pursuit of ever more integral stances toward reality. The ongoing battle between modernism and Romanticism subsumes a host of allied quarrels in the period—the academic versus the Beat, the establishment versus the underground, the conservative versus the liberal. With a fine sense of the national ethos, Philip Rahv divides American writers into "Palefaces," who are elegant and controlled, and "Redskins," who are intense and spontaneous. In a general way, the 1940s and 1950s belonged to a second wave of New Critics, who continued to uphold T. S. Eliot's notion that poetry is impersonal and to celebrate the virtues of formal coherence as demonstrated by Yeats, Frost, Stevens, and Auden. In reaction against such Apollonian aesthetics, the 1960s found an ancestor in Ezra Pound and his Dionysian indulgence of personality. Breaking free of both Eliot and Pound, the 1970s developed a sense of poetic emotion as inherently unfocused and quietly reflective, a poetry neither "cooked" nor "raw" in Robert Lowell's famous distinction, but al dente.

FORMALISTS/ACADEMIC POETS

As people of their time, the prewar poets who closed out their careers after the war tended to be formalists rather than improvisers. Conrad Aiken (1889–1973), E. E. Cummings (1894–1962), Babette Deutsch (1895–1982), Robert Frost (1874–1963), Horace Gregory (1898–1982), Archibald MacLeish (1892–1982), John Crowe Ransom (1888–1974), Wallace Stevens (1879–1955), Allen Tate (1899–1979), John Hall Wheelock (1886–1978)—all were so amenable to classroom explication that they formed the first generation of what has come to be known as "academic poets." An invidious term, *academic* suggests a poetry overly concerned with literary precedents, preciously intricate in its effects, hedged nervously with ironies and allusions. A number of poets whose reputation is postwar redeem the term. Like the best poets of the first generation, they bring a vigor to the academic mode that belies its reputation for chill formality and contextual irrelevance. Notable among them are Theodore Roethke (1908–1963), Elizabeth Bishop (1911–1979), Randall Jarrell (1914–1965), J. V. Cunningham (b. 1911), Howard Nemerov (b. 1920), Richard Wilbur (b. 1921), James Merrill (b. 1926), Adrienne Rich (b. 1929), May Swenson (b. 1919), Howard Moss (b. 1922), Daniel Hoffman (b. 1923), John Hollander (b. 1929), Richard Howard (b. 1929), Louise Glück (b. 1943), Anthony Hecht (b. 1923), John Fandel (b. 1925), Maxine Kumin (b. 1925), William Meredith (b. 1919), and David Slavitt (b. 1935).

Theodore Roethke once described his poems as "a kind of struggle out of the slime; part of a slow spiritual progress; an effort to be born, and later, to become something more." This evolutionary metaphor represents accurately the development of his postwar oeuvre. *The Lost Son* (1948) is a collection of poems in which Roethke plumbs the depths of Jungian consciousness and discovers a childhood world darkly fecund and damply green, alive with worms, snails, and toads, a world in which unreason and nature hold primordial sway. A sequence of poems begun in *The Lost Son*, continued in *Praise to the End!* (1951), and picked up again in *The Waking* (1953) delineates an evolutionary course upward. Psychic wholeness stands at the end of Roethke's evolutionism: the poems in *The Waking* have as their general subject a confrontation with selfhood; the poems in *The Far Field* (1964) proclaim the achievement of mystical self-realization. Like most poets who lay out a course from the primal swamp to mysticism, Roethke is most convincing at the lower depths, where the intensity of suffering that stands behind his creative act finds expression in sudden jolts of mood, lurching rhythms, broken phrases, thudding repetitions, and insistently concrete imagery. Indeed, Roethke's truest voice is a poetic rant with roots in both transcendentalism and Whitman's bardic rhapsody. More than any other formalist of his time, he recapitulated American's major poetic traditions and sowed the seeds of 1960s confessionalism.

At the time of her death in 1979, Elizabeth Bishop was among the most revered of contemporary American poets. In a modest but steady outpouring collected in *North & South* (1946), *A Cold Spring* (1955), *Questions of Travel* (1965), *The Complete Poems* (1969), and *Geography III* (1976), she turned accounts of the most incidental and particular experiences into sudden flashes of universal knowledge. She did so without rhetorical flourish and without what she would have regarded as immodest presence in her work. Her syntax is, like Marianne Moore's, virtually indistinguishable from prose syntax, and her diction is unpretentious, elegant only in its absolute accuracy. Yet the net effect of her poetry is luminously evocative and as shapely as it is impersonal—a very model of the formalist aesthetic. Resident for many years in Brazil, Bishop also played an important role in translating the major Brazilian writers and introducing them to a North American audience.

In a famous phrase, Robert Lowell once labeled Randall Jarrell "the most heartbreaking poet of his generation." Jarrell's generation was deeply savaged by World War II, and his early war poetry, collected in *Blood for a Stranger* (1942), *Little Friend, Little Friend* (1945), and *Losses* (1948), is seeped in a weltschmerz that the author never entirely justifies. Like some of the poems in *Losses*, many of the poems in *The Woman at the Washington Zoo* (1960) and *The Lost World* (1965) develop their peacetime weltschmerz through fairy tales, German ones in particular. Others evoke a Wordsworthian reverie in which reality and fantasy commingle. The innocence of childhood was unabashedly esteemed by Jarrell, but many of these later poems look back to childhood as a world in dark and febrile contact with terrible myths that can be recaptured now only in the reworkings of memory and imagination. Sentimentality dilutes the formalist rigor of his work as a result. Jarrell may ultimately be remembered more for his sensitive literary criticism and for a satiric novel about academe called *Pictures from an Institution* (1954) than for his flawed poetry.

J. V. Cunningham assumes an antimodernist stance in his postwar work, both in his poetry and in his fascinating treatise *The Quest of the Opal* (1950), which describes his development from pseudomodernist poetry to a more traditional poetry of statement. Classical verse forms, precise meters and rhymes, an unemphatic, discursive style, and a severe economy of presentation characterize the poems in *The Judge Is Fury* (1947) and *Doctor Drink* (1950), but these characteristics are relaxed in the sequence *To What Strangers, What Welcome* (1964). The epigram proves to be Cunningham's most natural form, and he is without question the most accomplished epigrammist writing in English in the postwar period. Indeed, the nuggets of statement in *Trivial, Vulgar and Exalted: Epigrams* (1957) evoke the epigrams of Ben Jonson in both spirit and style.

In the course of his career, Howard Nemerov gradually softens the self-conscious erudition and didacticism of his early poetry in favor of a more brooding posture. He retains, however, a formalist love for epigram and wit, for a combination of precise diction and syntax, and for the detachment, as he says, "of a single thought from its ambiguous surroundings." As a young poet, Nemerov was influenced by the modernism of John Crowe Ransom and Wallace Stevens, and his first book of poems, *The Image and the Law* (1947), reflects their gift for isolating the universal within a riot of awarenesses. In the poems of *The Salt Garden* (1955), he cultivates the naturalist's eye—notably in "The Goose Fish," his most elegantly melancholic poem. Touched by the issues of the 1960s, he cultivates in *The Next Room of the Dream* (1962) and *The Blue Swallows* (1967) a greater plainness of style and a more darkly satiric point of view. These characteristics carry over into *Gnomes & Occasions* (1973) and *The Western Approaches* (1975). Few midcentury poets can match Nemerov's variety, for he has written in an extraordinary number of verse forms, ranging from the epigram to blank verse. A graceful literary critic, he is also the author of *Poetry and Fiction* (1963), *Reflexions on Poetry & Poetics* (1972), and *Figures of Thought* (1978).

Richard Wilbur remains more entirely faithful to the formalist aesthetic than Nemerov. *The Beautiful Changes* (1947) and *Ceremony* (1950), his first collections, epitomize formalist sophistication and celebrate the redemption of a disorderly world by the power of beauty. In *Things of This World* (1956), he balances this abstract appreciation of beauty with a greater interest in physical objects, and in such poems as "A Baroque Wall-Fountain in the Villa Sciarra" and "For the New Railway Station in Rome," he writes his best poetry—graceful, allusive, intensely phrased, its lucid symmetries seeming to hold the world's chaos at bay. Wilbur's subsequent collections have been criticized for responding too little to the Vietnam years and to the postmodernist impulse. It it thought typical of his formalist detachment that *Walking to Sleep* (1969) contains a poem rebuking President Johnson not for presiding over the American involvement in Vietnam but for disdaining his official portrait. Yet Wilbur's critics make too much of his impersonality and detachment. His poems are entirely his own—sweet natured, witty, quietly attentive to the harmonies of existence. Wilbur is also a distinguished translator of Molière. His renderings of *The Misanthrope* (1955), *Tartuffe* (1963), *The School for Wives* (1972), and *The Learned Ladies* (1978) are among the most skillful translations in the language, rivaling the original French texts in both polish and wit.

Like Nemerov and Wilbur, James Merrill is a master of the standard poetic forms and the polished surface. The couplet, the quatrain, and even the sonnet sequence set the stage for delicate arabesques of statement and shapely meters in his work, from *First Poems* (1951) through a trilogy composed of

The Book of Ephraim (in *Divine Comedies*, 1976), *Mirabell: Books of Number* (1978), and *Scripts for the Pageant* (1980). Without abandoning any of his formalist polish, Merrill gradually loosens the reins of his earlier poetry, and in the trilogy that is his masterwork, he indulges the narrative impulse first evidenced in the poems of *The Country of a Thousand Years of Peace* (1959) and the autobiographical impulse evident in the poems of *Water Street* (1962). The trilogy is based on the system of the Ouija board. Composed in twenty-six sections labeled "A" through "Z," "The Book of Ephraim" uses up the letters of the board, while *Mirabel* exhausts the Ouija's numbers in ten books labeled from zero to nine. *Scripts for the Pageant* is left with the Ouija's elemental "Yes & No." A compendium of voices both in time and eternity, both individual and social, and awash with the flotsam of a memory fifty years old, the sequence illumines ways in which the variety of human experience orchestrates a human life and shapes memory. It invites comparison with Lowell's *History* and Berryman's *Dream Songs*, ultimately with Pound's *Cantos*.

Like Merrill, Adrienne Rich has found her way from a precocious formalism to a more autobiographical mode of poetry. *A Change of World* (1951) and *The Diamond Cutters* (1955) are impressive for their polished stanzas and metrics, but in light of Rich's later poetry, their formalist perfections seem an evasion of life. In *Snapshots of a Daughter-in-Law* (1963), she experimented with more personal statement and sounded the first conscious notes of a feminist *cri de coeur*. Both developments came to dominate her work in *Necessities of Life* (1966), *Leaflets* (1969), *The Will to Change* (1971), and *Diving into the Wreck* (1973). It seems inevitable that Rich should simultaneously have abandoned her tidily squared cadences and stanzas as if they were tantamount to housewifely neatness. The looser poetics of juxtaposition and lineation that replaces her formalism is to some degree a diminution of her art, but poems such as "Diving into the Wreck," "Cartographies of Silence," and "Meditations for a Savage Child" are passionately intelligent and complexly ordered, important less for their feminism than for their aesthetic realization. In her most recent poetry, notably in *The Dream of a Common Language* (1978) and *A Wild Patience Has Taken Me This Far* (1982), Rich seems to be moving beyond feminist anger to a more celebrative mode of statement and to a new integration of her poetic and moral impulses. She is a distinguished exception to the general rule that poet-activists make poor poets.

The poems of May Swenson have the well-tempered and finely polished surface admired by formalists but are more typographically inventive than the formalist norm permits. The effect of her visual inventiveness is extradimensional, for her spacial array of words and lines is wedded intimately to the poem's meaning and becomes as vital a mode of its elaboration as meter, rhyme, or image. Indeed, in her eight collections ranging from *Another Animal* (1954) to *New and Selected Things Taking Place* (1978), it is Swenson's distinction that her visual effects always supplement such basic craftsmanship, never supplanting it, as tends to be the case in the work of Mary Ellen Solt (b. 1920), Richard Kostelanetz (b. 1940), and other "concrete" poets who made a stir in the 1960s. At her best, Swenson invests ordinary phenomena with metaphysical mystery. Eggs, suns, blankets, kites, waves, trains, even DNA molecules become the focus of a perception so attentive to iconographic mysteries, so playful in its conceits, that her epistemological queries seem paradoxically tactile and sensuous. Appositely, the riddle is one of her favorite and most successful forms.

Although his iambic rhythms have loosened over the years and his penchant for the abstract has surrendered some ground to the concrete, Howard Moss remains a formalist poet writing in the tradition of Wallace Stevens and W. H. Auden. In exemplary collections like *Finding Them Lost* (1965) and *Selected Poems* (1971), his poetry is fastidiously precise in its diction, and wry, clever, and urbane in its tone. Although preoccupied with such appreciable subjects as mutability in the self and in the New York cityscape, Moss fails to engage major attention. His love of wordplay seems recherché to some tastes, his echoes of Stevens and Auden empty imitation.

Better known as a critic than as a poet, Daniel Hoffman deserves more recognition than he has received for his carefully measured verses. His poems tend to place the quest for a significant personal life in the context of the rituals and myths that underlie all human experience, much in the mode of his criticism. In the poetry of *An Armada of Thirty Whales* (1954), *A Little Geste* (1960), and *The City of Satisfactions* (1963), he labors myth too insistently, perhaps, but displays a happy facility for mixing irony and seriousness and for images freshly minted from experience. His more recent collections, such as *Broken Laws* (1970), *The Center of Attention* (1974), and an extended sequence on William Penn entitled *Brotherly Love* (1981), merit respect for their technical virtuosity and their quiet, deeply humanistic affirmations.

Writing in one of the highest styles of any recent American poet, John Hollander brings a virtuoso intelligence and an Audenesque sensibility to contemporary subjects that pale almost into insignificance beneath the awesome weight of his technique. Literary, mythic, philosophical, and religious allusions have a neoclassical density in his work from the first, and the allusiveness of *A Crackling of Thorns* (1958), *Visions from the Ramble* (1965), and *The Night Mirror* (1971) becomes even more dense and intimidating in *Tales Told of the Fathers* (1975), *Spectral Emanations* (1978), and *Blue Wine and Other Poems* (1979). Some of the more artificial stratagems of Hollander's technique are abandoned in the poetry after *Visions from the Ramble*, but a daunting technical brilliance and an allusive intellectuality remain its considerable strength. These qualities are no less the poetry's weakness, for the cost of mastering Hollander's rococo elaborations of wit, form, and intellect is sometimes disproportionate to its aesthetic quantum.

An accomplished translator of more than 150 books, Richard Howard is also accomplished in the art of writing dra-

matic monologues. *Untitled Subjects* (1969) is a collection of
fifteen such poems that attempt to crystallize key moments in
nineteenth-century sensibility. Howard has a portraitist's
sense of the revealing angle and a historian's sense of period
detail. He catches Richard Strauss, fresh from Debussy's opera
Pelléas et Mélisande, suggesting that Arnold Schoenberg write
the symphonic poem *Pelleas und Melisande*; catches Lady Tre-
velyan informing her son that she erred in giving him her Mac-
aulay papers; catches Gladstone's secretary indiscreetly char-
acterizing his employer. *Two-Part Inventions* (1974) is a collection of dialogues as imaginatively devised. It includes Oscar
Wilde talking with Walt Whitman in Camden, Edith Wharton
disputing with Gerald Roseman as to which of them had been
more truly Gerald Mackenzie's lover. Such poems and others
like them in *Fellow Feelings* (1976) and *Misgivings* (1979) succeed brilliantly in realizing Howard's intention to recoup for
poetry "energy that has leaked into fiction, into theatre." A
poet of great technical competence, he also comes closest of any
contemporary poet to equaling Auden's skill in syllabic verse.
labic verse.

Louise Glück writes most often about familial agonies—
about the death of children, about love and its failures, and
about motherhood and its slow march from intimacy to es-
trangement. The most interesting aspect of her work is its interaction of thematic obliquity and formal control. This interaction gives rise to an aura of mysterious encodement, both in
the angry poems of *Firstborn* (1968) and in the more resigned
and melancholy poems of *The House on Marshland* (1975). Indeed, her best poems draw their strength from half-articulated
situations to which her personae respond with a consciousness
caught between trauma and Freudian understanding. Hers is
a poetry not only of half lights but also of half effects: of
rhythms half metrical and half prosaic, of voices midway between lyric and narrative, of aural patterns shot through with
half rhymes. Glück has a sense all her own of the oblique statement and its aesthetic realization, but Wallace Stevens seems

a general influence on her poetry, and William Blake seems a particular influence on a sequence of linked poems in *The Garden* (1976).

Anthony Hecht is a conservator of literary traditions in several important ways, but most notably in his formalist commitment to an elevated diction, to elaborate metrical organizations, and to stanzas both rhyme-crossed and shapely. He has also an affinity for evoking literary precedents. His "Le Masseur de Ma Soeur" is a witty play on Wallace Stevens's "La Monocle de Mon Oncle"; his "Dover Bitch" is an ironic answer to Matthew Arnold's "Dover Beach"; and his "Rites and Ceremonies" and "The Venetian Vespers" seem reworkings of T. S. Eliot's *Four Quartets* and "Gerontion." The polished surface and patrician tone of the virtuoso pieces in Hecht's first collection of poems, *A Summoning of Stones* (1954), represent still another kind of literary conservatism—a commemoration of his formal tutelage by John Crowe Ransom and more informal tutelage by Allen Tate. But Hecht's subsequent collections, *The Hard Hours* (1967), *Millions of Strange Shadows* (1977), and *The Venetian Vespers* (1979), sound a deeper note than the ironic lyricism of Ransom and Tate. Many of the poems in these later volumes give voice to anarchic, deep-toned emotions born of a pessimism that admits no compromise with the horrors of humanity's condition. History seems to speak to Hecht of nothing but human suffering, from the death of the Emperor Valarian to the mass deaths in Buchenwald. The formal control of language and vision are his breakwater against such tidal chaos, "a grace won," he says, "from all losses."

John Fandel has a poetic sensibility so measured, so quietly reverent, that his poems seek a kind of awed silence. Brevity and formal polish are his hallmarks; a pantheistic note sounded in the presence of birdsong, falls of the sea, and the Christian mysteries is his most successful inflection. "Nature and art, and all that—and for all that,/ still, the only likely going twosome, even though/ these two are so unlikely a couple," he muses. "Bach/ and a catbird?—Bach and a catbird." Verbally playful and in love with the oblique pun, he adds a

dash of motley to his Robert Frost corduroys in the collections
Testament (1959), *Body of Earth* (1972), *The Deserted Green-
house* (1974), and *Bach and a Catbird* (1978) and wears the
ensemble with a dandy's sureness of taste. An aphoristic min-
imalism seems to attract him in recent years, notably in *Saun-
tering* (1975), but the meditative lyric best suits his contemplative cast of mind.

Maxine Kumin's remarks on her craft would align her with
the formalists even if her poems did not. "You begin with the
chaos of impressions and feelings, this aura that overtakes you,
that forces you to write," she says. "And, in the process of writing, as you marshall your arguments, as you marshall your
metaphors really, as you pound and hammer the poem into
shape and into form, the order—the marvelous informing order
emerges from it." In *Halfway* (1961), her first collection, she
brings a mature technical competence to bear in poems about
achieving personal identity and bearing deeply grieved losses.
Growing into a Jewish identity receives special emphasis in
the autobiographical poems of *The Privilege* (1965), as does the
death of her father in *The Nightmare Factory* (1970). *Up Country* (1972), *House, Bridge, Fountain, Gate* (1975), and *The Re-
trieval System* (1978) are more concerned with fixing details
and properly naming homey things like houses, bridges, and
country gates. Such fixing and naming become important acts
of control in Kumin's dream- and death-haunted world, important certainties among her questions about nature, family,
and human administration of the world. A modest and unsentimental poet, she radiates a sanity as great as her technical
proficiency.

William Meredith's first success was with twelve war
poems in *Love Letter from an Impossible Land* (1944). His subsequent collections, *Ships and Other Figures* (1948), *The Open
Sea* (1958), and *The Wreck of the Thresher* (1964), also evoke
images of sailors and airmen, but in such elaborately patterned
verse and in so erudite an idiom that their emotional strength
is generally thought muffled. Without abandoning any of his
precision or grace, Meredith has adopted in more recent poems

a looseness of syntax and a conversational idiom that accommodate better his elegant, quietly original meditations. *Hazard, the Painter* (1975) is his most impressive work. A sequence of sixteen poems, it is both a composite portrait of one artist's struggle to complete a painting and a long meditation on every artist's struggle against age, impotence, and the self. Ultimately, it authenticates what Meredith calls "accountable eyes"—an integrity of vision that seems for him both a moral and an aesthetic passion.

David Slavitt begins to write poetry in as hermetic a vein as Meredith, and, like him, he develops an affinity for the poetic sequence. The poems in *Suits for the Dead* (1961), *The Carnivore* (1965), *Child's Play* (1972), and *Vital Signs* (1975) are elegantly metrical and intricately architectural, but none of them attempts the antihermetical play of Slavitt's translations of the *Eclogues* (1971) and *Georgics* (1972), which juggle straight translation, critical interpretation, commentary, summary, and even his own persona as translator in an audacious imitation of what Slavitt calls the "exhilarating whipsaw" of Virgil's own effects. The title sequence of *Rounding the Horn* (1978) attempts a kind of suprahermetical play, however, in a series of twenty-four octaves climaxed by a sonnet. Each unit is a finished poem in itself; each, a knot in a tangled skein of thought. *Dozens* (1981) is still more ambitious: a sequence of 144 twelve-line stanzas that interweave the strands of some half-dozen stories. Inasmuch as Slavitt is a writer of extraordinary finish and variety, the critical neglect of his work is inexplicable.

When a poetics of openness and improvisation began to seem more relevant to American life in the 1960s than a poetics of shapeliness and closure, the formalist poem fell into critical disrepute. Nevertheless, any number of fine poets have continued to uphold the formalist aesthetic. Not so doctrinaire as the generation of formalists before them, they are willing to loosen their meters and rhymes, even to forsake them, but unwilling to forsake altogether traditional modes of craftsmanship.

The varieties and degrees of formalism in such poets are many. John Frederick Nims (b. 1913) has revivified the sonnet sequence and the epigram; Richard Hugo (1923–1982), the letter poem; David Wagoner (b. 1926), the instructional poem; and Louis Coxe (b. 1918), the dramatic monologue. Peter Davison (b. 1928) and Henry Taylor (b. 1942) have written important narrative verse. In a relatively small but impressive body of work, Carolyn Kizer (b. 1925) rejects what she calls "the sad sonneteers, toast-and-teasdales," and writes a tough-minded poetry distinguished for its technical elegance. Donald Justice (b. 1925) and Peter Meinke (b. 1932) achieve a commensurate elegance with sonnets, villanelles, and sestinas—Justice in a slightly archaic diction, Meinke in a contemporary idiom enlivened with humor and wit. Cid Corman's (b. 1924) and Edgar Bower's (b. 1924) poems have limited emotional range but are admirably chiseled and spare. Reed Whittemore (b. 1919) turns his refined sense of metrics to the service of light verse.

Several poets who began their careers as formalists have turned gradually to looser modes of writing, not always with greater success. William Dickey's (b. 1928) early poetry has a honed sardonicism and a comprehensive, formalist control, especially in *Of the Festivity* (1959) and *Interpreter's House* (1963). The nine long poems of *Rivers of the Pacific Northwest* (1969) are impressive in a looser mode, but *More under Saturn* (1971) and *The Rainbow Grocery* (1978) seem self-indulgently cynical and poetically frenzied. Donald Hall's (b. 1928) poetry in *Exiles & Marriages* (1955) is wrought of regular meters and rhymes, but Hall suppresses such conscious modes of control in favor of an alogical "Vatic Voice" in *A Roof of Tiger Lilies* (1964) and subsequent collections. His success with that voice is irregular but occasionally brilliant. Paul Zimmer's (b. 1934) work has evolved from the cerebral and carefully impersonal poems of *A Seed on the Wind* (1960) to casting himself as a persona in *The Republic of Many Voices* (1969) and *The Zimmer Poems* (1976).

Although arguably a modernist himself, William Carlos Williams (1883–1963) is a chief figure in the postmodern opposition to academic formalism. Against traditional metrics, an esoteric vocabulary, the time-honored subjects of poetry and their implied planes of consciousness, he counterpointed a sinuous, three-stepped line, a demotic idiom, and a kinesthetic engagement in the American scene. Many of his poems written between the world wars and the short poems published in *The Desert Music* (1954), *Journey to Love* (1955), and *Pictures from Brueghel* (1962) have an almost photographic instantaneousness, both in their descriptive bent and in their attempt to arrest perceptual experience. As such, they link themselves to characteristic work of the Black Mountain, San Francisco, and confessional poets—indeed, to the whole spectrum of postmodern improvisation.

But it was through the extended sequence *Paterson* (1946–1963) that Williams most firmly impressed his influence. In a collage deeply indebted to the techniques of modern painting, he viewed Paterson, New Jersey through bits of history, old letters, overheard conversations, news clippings, lyrical *aperçu*, and narrative passages about a host of real and imaginary characters. His theme in the poem is the human being and the city, and his discovery, as he said, is divorce—divorce from the land, from history, and from human fellowship. His achievement was to make poetry out of an improvisational interaction between the raw material of his understanding and his innumerable acts of perception as they flowed toward realization. No contemporary poet has charted that interaction more attractively.

Like Williams, Louis Zukofsky (1904–1978) began his poetic career as a modernist, but he emerged in the postwar period as a poet of process. Developmental, all-embracing, ultimately obscure and private, he moved from an aesthetic he called "objectification" to autobiographical meditation on such universal themes as marriage, fatherhood, and death. The long poem "*A*" (1978) dominates his oeuvre. A half-century in the writing, it is a work of forbidding difficulty, especially in the last twelve of its twenty-four sections, which are characterized by so improvisational a technique that Zukofsky tends to be read only by fellow poets and recondite academics. Indeed, the subtlety of the poem's imaginative organization and the occasional impenetrability of its syntax render "*A*" one of the most difficult works in postwar literature. Like *Finnegans Wake*, it bespeaks genius but awaits commensurate elucidation.

BLACK MOUNTAINISTS

Between 1951 and 1956, the poet Charles Olson (1910–1970) served as rector of the experimental Black Mountain College in North Carolina, and he brought together during that period an extraordinary group of avant-garde artists: the musicians John Cage and David Tudor, the choreographer and dancer Merce Cunningham, the painters Josef Albers and Robert Rauschenberg, the architect and futurist Buckminster Fuller, the poets Robert Creeley (b. 1926) and Robert Duncan (b. 1919). Edward Dorn (b. 1929), Joel Oppenheimer (b. 1930), and Jonathan Williams (b. 1929) studied at the college under this extraordinary faculty, and other poets were drawn to an informal association with the college through its sponsorship of the journals *Black Mountain Review* and *Origin*, most notably Denise Levertov (b. 1923).

Olson's commitment to a postmodern aesthetic was the inspiriting force of Black Mountain College in this arcadian period. In an influential essay entitled "Projective Verse" (1950), he drew analogously on the force-field theory of modern physics and argued that a poem is a "high-energy construct" in which "the perception must immediately and directly lead to a further perception." The sound and the sense of a poem interact, he maintained, as in a kinetic field, and the poet introduces a personal kinesis into the poem by orchestrating its lines to the rhythm of his actual breathing. Like Ezra Pound before him, Olson invoked scientific principles (which he may not have fully understood) to validate a dismissal of intellection, abstraction, and cognition in favor of a neo-Romantic primitivism.

Olson's achievement as a poet rests largely on two works, "The Kingfishers" (1949) and *The Maximus Poems* (1960–75). Like *The Waste Land*, a poem it seeks to answer and transcend, "The Kingfishers" balances a noble past against a mercantile present and incorporates snatches of quotations from other languages. In its profound feeling for an American past, its vast architectonics, and its moments of lyric beauty, it looks forward to *The Maximus Poems*, a sequence of more than 300 "letters" and "songs" in which the persona styles himself Maximus (after the second-century philosopher Maximus of Tyre) and slowly reveals himself as Olson. The songs and letters focus on the town of Gloucester, Massachusetts—its beginnings and growth, its evolving culture, and the poet's involvement in the town, both literal and symbolic. Like Williams's *Paterson*, a work that it recalls, *The Maximus Poems* is a work of cultural archeology as well as a major poetic sequence.

Concerned like Olson to reground poetry in human physiology, Robert Creeley dismisses a poem's form as "what happens" and affects a bare, laconic mode of statement in an effort to be true, moment by moment, to the fluctuations of his sensibility. His best work is in the collection *For Love* (1962), the typical poem of which is a free-verse improvisation so minimal in form and statement as to seem antiverbal. He brings wry humor and refined irony to poems about erotic feeling, particularly about married love, and his best poems characteristically seem fields of energy in which a few phrases highly charged with suggestiveness electrify the whole. Because he strips himself of a poet's arsenal of technique in order to remain true to his impulses, Creeley often seems to mutter without purpose, as in *Words* (1965) and *Pieces* (1968), the titles of which reflect an increasing truncation of statement. *A Day Book* (1972) and *Hello: A Journal* (1978) are compendia of prose and verse wherein he poises himself on the very edge of poetic statement.

Robert Duncan's poetry is as prolix as Creeley's is terse. A poet of wide and intelligent reading, he draws familiarly cupon occult interests, Platonism, the *Oxford English Dictio-*

nary, and classical Greek literature, and he is capable of alluding in a single poem to William Blake, Jakob Böhme, Thomas Carlyle, John Adams, Victor Hugo, and Dante. "I don't seek a synthesis," he says, "but a melee." Two long sequences of poems entitled "The Structure of Rhyme" and "Passages" constitute his major work. Arrayed among other poems in *The Opening of the Field* (1960) and *Bending the Bow* (1968), they attempt to be truly open-ended sequences, without coda, conclusion, or even continuity of print. "The Structure of Rhyme" is an unrhymed epic of a poet's development; "Passages" is a shamanistic work. Both are preeminently "field" poems, for their linguistic energy is unfettered, their allusiveness is unpruned, and their erotic-aesthetical sensibility is capacious. It is difficult to like such uncontrolled verse unless the reader shares its mystique of Whiteheadian process, but there can be no question that Duncan is a gifted poet.

Edward Dorn, one of the poets nurtured by Black Mountain College, writes in a variety of modes but is best known for long narrative meditations such as the title poems in *From Gloucester Out* (1964), *Idaho Out* (1965), and *The North Atlantic Turbine* (1967). His most memorable work of this kind is the Gunslinger volumes (collected as *Slinger* in 1975), a surrealistic cowboy epic that broadly parodies the Western genre but asks serious questions about American values beneath its camp conceits and comic-strip dialogue. Dorn's tone is more reverential in *Recollections of Gran Apachería* (1974), a collection of his poems and thoughts on the Apache Indians and the fate of their tribe. Increasingly a social satirist, Dorn seems preoccupied with peoples overlooked or oppressed. His translations of poems by José Elimio Pacheco, César Vallejo, and other Latin American poets are an extension of that concern.

Joel Oppenheimer's poetry suggests an indebtedness more to William Carlos Williams's "flat" line than to Olson's forcefield aesthetic, but Olson played a key role in Oppenheimer's development when he encouraged the young poet to indulge a discursive bent. The result is a body of poetry unhurried in manner and direct in statement—an oeuvre that seems to say we have had enough of modernist subtlety, elegance, and compression. Oppenheimer never veers from his commitment to humanistic values, but many of his poems in *The Love Bit* (1962), *In Time* (1969), *On Occasion* (1973), and *names, dates, & places* (1978) could pass for studies in disengagement, so gently, so unconstrainedly do they reveal that commitment.

But Jonathan Williams is the most unconstrained of the Black Mountain poets. The title of *Strung Out with Elgar on a Hill* (1970) suggests both the effervescence of his work and his broad interest in music and musical effects. *The Empire Finals at Verona* (1959) contains a series of poems that translate Catullus into the argot of American jazz, while his much-admired *Mahler* poems (1969) are written one each to the movements of Gustav Mahler's symphonies. The poems in *Blues & Roots/Rue & Bluets* (1971) orchestrate rural Appalachian speech into a folk fantasia as witty as it is linguistically melodious. There is a darker side to Williams, evident in "Excavations from the Case-Histories of Havelock Ellis" (1972), but he is most successful in a mood of energetic brightness.

It is conventional to place Denise Levertov among the Black Mountain poets, largely because some of her early poetry was published under their aegis, and also because she once proclaimed Duncan and Creeley the most important poets among her contemporaries. Nonetheless, Levertov's poetry transcends the Black Mountain school. She shares with Duncan an ancestral interest in mysticism, but she is more caught up than he in the quotidian. She shares with Creeley a tendency to chronicle the passing phases of her awareness, but she embraces a wider range of experience than he. Abundantly manifest in the collections *Here and Now* (1957), *The Jacob's Ladder* (1961), and *O Taste and See* (1964), her typical poem is a free-verse construct in which the act of perception is so intense that it becomes a realization uncluttered with logic, both quietly mystifying and deeply spiritual. Its form is instinctive but controlled—hard wrung but seemingly effortless. "Form is never more than *revelation* of content," she says, correcting Creeley's notion that form is only an extension of content. Levertov's social protest and Vietnam poems, collected in *The Sorrow Dance* (1967), *Relearning the Alphabet* (1970), and *To Stay Alive* (1971), are less successful than her more purely lyrical poems because they are tinged with sentimentality and polemic, but a series of poems on the death of her older sister, "The Olga Poems," gives distinction to the last of these volumes and serves as a bridge to the more rounded perceptions in *Footprints* (1972), *The Freeing of the Dust* (1975), and *Life in the Forest* (1978).

SAN FRANCISCANS/BEATS

At the same time that the Black Mountain campus was asserting its rejection of traditional poetics, San Francisco was becoming a mecca for young poets fleeing the poet-professor mold and seeking relief from orthodox pieties. Long an antiformalist, the poet Kenneth Rexroth (1905–1982) welcomed the young poets to California and declared them his heirs, but they soon outgrew his patronage and launched a cult of absolute freedom in both their life-styles and their poetics. Less a movement than a gathering of free spirits, they issued no manifestos but tended in time to merge with the Beats, enriching the Beat movement with their blend of Leftist politics and oriental mysticism, their worship of sex and the orgasm, and their affectation of childhood simplicity. The most important poet to have emerged from this San Francisco renaissance is Allen Ginsberg (b. 1926). Others who figure prominently in the renaissance are Lawrence Ferlinghetti (b. 1919?), Gary Snyder (b. 1930), William Everson (b. 1912), James Broughton (b. 1913), Jack Spicer (1925–1965), Gregory Corso (b. 1930), and Richard Brautigan (b. 1935). Robert Duncan enters the San Francisco scene after the demise of Black Mountain College in 1956; Diane di Prima (b. 1934) joins the scene in 1968.

Ginsberg's poem "Howl" (1956) is the holy writ of Beat poetry—a long, agonized outcry against an America that subverts the "holy" impulses of its young men and drives them to excesses of drug addiction, alcoholism, and sex. "I saw the best minds of my generation destroyed," the poet-speaker begins, and he goes on to develop a catalogue of examples that shock and horrify the reader. Although the poem has obvious antecedents in Whitman and the populist revolutionism of an earlier day, it evokes more strongly a Hebraic tradition of denunciation and prophecy. It is preeminently an oral poem, meant to be declaimed. "Ideally, each line of *Howl* is a single breath unit," Ginsberg has said in echo of Olson, and he conceives the difficult length of his lines as an injunction to his reader "to mouth more madly." At a time when poetry was essentially a written, scholarly art, Ginsberg and the Beats restored it to bardic madness and the stage.

"Kaddish for Naomi Ginsberg 1894–1956," the title poem of *Kaddish, and Other Poems* (1961), is Ginsberg's masterpiece. An elegiac commemoration of his mother, it interweaves oblique fragments of Hebrew prayer and expressions of the poet's own feelings with terrible recollections of her psychotic paranoia, her confinement in a mental institution, her cancer, and her death. The emotional stratification of the poem, its composite horror and tenderness, justifies Ginsberg's rant to a degree unequaled in his other work. Indeed, the poems in *Reality Sandwiches* (1963), *Planet News* (1968), *The Fall of America: Poems of These States* (1972), and *Mind Breaths* (1978) represent a lessening of the hallucinatory grandeur and almost unbearably affecting tension of "Howl" and "Kaddish."

Through his City Lights Bookshop and Press in San Francisco, Lawrence Ferlinghetti has done more than anyone else to provide Beat writers with a forum for their countercultural art. Renowned for avant-garde poetry readings and the distinguished audiences that they drew, his bookstore was the unofficial center of the Beat movement, and his Pocket Poet series of publications is distinguished not only by the poems of Robert Duncan, Philip Lamantia (b. 1925), Denise Levertov, and Gregory Corso, but by the famous edition of Ginsberg's *Howl, and Other Poems* that resulted in Ferlinghetti's trial in 1957 for publishing obscene literature. Ferlinghetti's own poetry is probably less important to literary history than his patronage of Ginsberg and other San Francisco poets, but it is by no means negligible. As part of his purpose to move poetry "back into the streets where it once was," his poems are highly readable and rapid paced, a long sinuous flow on the page, irreverent, disingenuous, both winsome and wry. He is most successful with the poems of *A Coney Island of the Mind* (1958), the most sweet tempered of his books. The political and societal passions that tend to dominate his other volumes strike a harsher, less engaging note.

Gary Snyder is the only Beat poet to approach Ginsberg's stature, but his interests range beyond the San Francisco scene and have led him to work as a lumberjack, forester, seaman, scholar of oriental languages, and student of Zen Buddhism. All these endeavors have left their mark on his deceptively simple poetry. From the East he takes a contemplative inwardness and a diction so imagistic and lean that it evokes the haiku. From his experiences as a laborer, he derives a passion for ecological balance in the High Sierras and Arizona desert. The play of his orientalized mind on images of the American West is evident in *Riprap* (1959), his first collection of poems, but is more perfectly achieved in *Myths and Texts* (1960), a long, complex poem that places the texts of civilized society in opposition to the myths of primitive cultures and finds the former inadequate. In *Turtle Island* (1974) and the published sections of *Mountains and Rivers without End*, a vast sequence-in-progress, Snyder's work is more polemical in tone than before, but with concomitant gains in control, self-confidence, and maturity. Despite his Romantic primitivism, he is a deeply sophisticated poet.

In a now-famous essay called "San Francisco Letter" (1957), Kenneth Rexroth heralded the Beat poets as a vibrant new voice in the land and drew attention to William Everson as "perhaps the most profoundly moving and durable of the poets of the San Francisco Renaissance." A lay brother at that time in the Dominican order, publishing as "Brother Antoninus," Everson gained a larger and more sophisticated audience through Rexroth's endorsement than he would otherwise have had. He quickly abandoned the sometimes embarrassing pieties of his early religious verse in favor of spiritual autobiography. *The Hazards of Holiness* (1962) and *The Rose of Solitude* (1967) chronicle his gathering unease as a monk; *Man-Fate* (1974) and *The Masks of Drought* (1979) chronicle his break with the Dominican order in 1969 and his concurrent readjustments of thought and feeling. Never a fully competent craftsman, he continues to gain his best effects through emotional and rhetorical excesses.

James Broughton is somewhat better known as an experimental filmmaker than as a poet but has earned a small reputation for his lyrical celebrations of the self. The business of poets, he says, "is to ignite a revolution of insight in the soul." He sparks that revolution in his own work with fabulistic imaginings, Mother Goose stylistics, and a pristine belief in love. "Songs for Anxious Children" is the appropriate subtitle of *Musical Chairs* (1950), his second volume of poems, but the phrase describes equally well the poems in *Ballad of Mad Jenny* (1949), *An Almanac for Amorists* (1955), and *Tidings* (1965), which are characterized no less than the poems in *Musical Chairs* by visionary images drawn in the bright, primary colors of childhood. *True and False Unicorn* (1957) is Broughton's most impressive work. A long poem in four parts, its structure is a unicorn's search to discover whether he is "fantasy or flesh," whether his passions are "mock or real." The fabulous animal's slow progress from self-doubt to self-affirmation is an adroit vehicle for Broughton's celebration of unreason, individuality, and the liberating force of the imagination.

As a student of linguistics, Jack Spicer was troubled by the disjunction between language and its referents and came to believe that the poet's task was to minimize that disjunction by cultivating an extreme passivity in the creative process. Like Blake and Yeats before him, he believed "voices" dictated his poems, and his goal after the mid-1950s was apparently to collapse his own authorship into spirit-authorship. In pursuit of his goal, he eliminated such barriers to that collapse as rhyme and the first-person pronoun; ultimately, it would seem, he sought to eliminate purpose and cognitive sense altogether. The first, tentative step toward this collapse into spirit-authorship is *After Lorca* (1957), a collection of poems ostensibly introduced by the dead García Lorca himself. Although increasingly obscure and sometimes pretentious, *Billy the Kid* (1959), *The Heads of the Town up to the Aether* (1962), *The Holy Grail* (1964), and *Language* (1965) are not without interest. Purpose and form escaped Spicer even when he cultivated unreason and chance.

Gregory Corso's violent, unworked poetry merits little attention in itself, but its endorsement by such key figures of the Beat movement as Ginsberg, Kerouac, and Ferlinghetti gives it a paraliterary significance. A veteran of the criminal courts, Corso is eminently street-wise but essentially a naïf—the sort of wild child the Beats tended to regard as messianic. His poems set up the poet as a seer and oppose him to the America of technocrats, industrialists, and warmongers. The messianic vision is all: "If the poet's mind is shapely," he cries, "then his poem will come out shapely!" The poems in *Gasoline* (1958), *The Happy Birthday of Death* (1960), *Long Live Man* (1962), and *Elegiac Feelings American* (1970) belie that confidence. Crudely structured, stylistically gauche, alternately sententious and banal, they shriek their impassioned confusions and improvised faiths. They are perhaps the most extreme example of the Beat reluctance to let raw potential mature into art.

Richard Brautigan's poetry mimics the naiveté of Corso's but with a success born of literary sophistication. Brautigan's method is to maintain his stylistics at such an elementary level that his pared sentences seem logically incontrovertible, his bald analogies inexplicably luminous. The faux naïf conceit is his trademark, as suggested by the titles *The Galilee Hitch-Hiker* (1958), *Lay the Marble Tea* (1959), *The Octopus Frontier* (1960), and *All Watched Over by Machines of Loving Grace* (1967). But such dispassionate whimsy satisfies Brautigan less in the 1970s than in the 1960s. In *Rommel Drives On Deep into Egypt* (1970) he turns more directly than before to social commentary; in *Loading Mercury with a Pitchfork* (1976) he allows himself a new darkness of mood; and in *June 30th, June 30th* (1978) he is overtly autobiographical for the first time.

In its serial assimilation of the Beats, the hippies, the flower children, the war protesters, and the feminists, and in its geographical reach even to New York City's bohemian neighborhoods, the community of San Francisco poets has developed considerable breadth. The work of Diane di Prima illumines that breadth. A resident of Greenwich Village until 1968, when she relocated on the West Coast, di Prima was coeditor during the 1960s of a New York City-based monthly entitled *Floating Bear* that featured the poetry of the San Francisco writers. Her own poetry reveals interests that parallel the San Franciscans', from the Beat hallucinations of her *New Handbook of Heaven* (1963), to the political engagement of her *Revolutionary Letters* (1971), to the feminist awareness of her *Loba* poems (Parts 1–8, 1978). Such an attachment to the San Francisco scene suggests that the Bay Area is not just a mecca for experimentalists, but a countercultural state of mind.

CONFESSIONALISTS

The greatest challenge to the formalism of the 1950s came from a group of poets who revealed the most painful truths about themselves, partly in self-administered therapy for psychoses real or imagined, partly in the conviction that the age called for such candor. Their work was dubbed "confessional" poetry on the publication of Robert Lowell's *Life Studies* in 1959, and the name has adhered. Because it places the poet's suffering at the center of concern, confessional poetry is often understood as just another bypath of Romanticism. But the centrality of the traditional Romantic poet to his poem implies a high valuation of his individual being and of human individuality as such. The confessional poet has less self-esteem. Clinically fascinated by the symptoms of his own psychosis, he has little urge to moralize his condition or to move it toward resolution. At his best, he takes us to a point just this side of madness and engages us in the danse macabre of voyeurism turned inward.

Improvised stanzaic forms, jagged syntax, and clotted metrics are the confessionalists' badge of sincerity. Standing behind such poetics are experiments of the Black Mountainists and the Beats, the publication of Williams's *Paterson*, and, preeminently, the publication of Pound's Cantos—the *Pisan Cantos* in 1948, the *Rock Drill* in 1956, and the *Thrones* in 1959. Robert Lowell (1917–1977) and John Berryman (1914–1972) were the most accomplished of the confessional poets, and together they did more to change poetic sensibility than any other poets of their generation. Other important confessionalists include W. D. Snodgrass (b. 1926), Anne Sexton (1928–1974), and Sylvia Plath (1932–1963). Blurring at its edges into autobiographical poetry, the confessional movement might also be considered to encompass such poets as Clayton Eshleman (b. 1935), Sandra Hochman (b. 1936), Stanley Plumly (b. 1939), Marvin Bell (b. 1937), and William Heyen (b. 1940).

Robert Lowell's writing affected from the first a strained syntax and a tone of smoldering fury. The poems of *Land of Unlikeness* (1944) and *Lord Weary's Castle* (1946) are tense with the strain of applying his convert-Catholicism to the spirit of an age "unhouseled by Geveva's night." The seven dramatic monologues in *The Mills of the Kavanaughs* (1951) also strain for effect but point to the easier, more prosaic manner of *Life Studies* (1959). It was Lowell's psychiatrist who suggested he write the journal of his childhood experiences that became "91 Revere Street," a prose memoir at the heart of *Life Studies*, and a psychoanalytic impulse to probe the dark recesses of awareness seems to have carried over into accompanying poems about Lowell's boyhood, his Boston Brahmin family, his marriage to Elizabeth Hardwick, and his confinements as conscientious objector and mental patient. But *Life Studies* also contains poems that depict a larger world hastening toward apocalypse. Indeed, it is the assimilation of America's cultural and political malaise into his own confessions that gives Lowell's poems their characteristic urgency.

Since the publication of *Life Studies*, Lowell has generally been acknowledged as the strongest and most original voice in postwar American poetry. But *Life Studies* proved somewhat more of a turning point for poetry than for Lowell himself, inasmuch as his venture into personal epic was only part of a restless search for models to contain his muttering style. Having established himself as a master of provisional rhythms and forms, he did not return to them in the same degree until *Day by Day* (1977), his last collection. He turned to couplet-quatrains in *Near the Ocean* (1967), to unrhymed sonnet-stanzas in *Notebook 1967–68* (1969). The last is a diaristic sequence of poems that he recast a year later into *Notebook* (1970) and finally into the first two volumes of the trilogy *For Lizzie and Harriet, History*, and *The Dolphin* (1973). He was in the habit not only of recasting poems he had already published, but of versifying prose and translating poetry not his own. Sentences from Hawthorne, Jonathan Edwards, Elizabeth Bishop, and Mary McCarthy are the bases of poems in *For the Union Dead* (1964); renderings of Horace and Juvenal are a large part of *Near the Ocean*. But in all the modes of Lowell's poetry, the free association remains his driving, dangerous, most interesting force. Saved from incoherence by an absolute precision of wording and a magisterial intelligence, it gives his renderings of history and private experience an extraordinary drama.

John Berryman's first verse, collected in *Poems* (1942) and *The Dispossessed* (1948), are impersonal exercises in irony and paradox very much in the vein of 1940s poetry. But in the same decade he wrote a sequence of 115 Petrarchan sonnets (published in 1967 as *Berryman's Sonnets*) that chronicle an adulterous love affair with such candor that the poems seem a first breath of the confessional spirit. The long poem *Homage to Mistress Bradstreet* (1956) also borders on the confessional. Ostensibly a biographical meditation on the Puritan poet Anne Bradstreet, it is an astonishingly libidinal performance in its merging of Berryman's consciousness with Bradstreet's, even as he engages her in conversation and imagines her his mistress. The technique of *Homage to Mistress Bradstreet* led to *77 Dream Songs* (1964) and Dream Songs 78–385 in *His Toy, His Dream, His Rest* (1968), an open-ended sequence of poems in which Berryman merges with a multipersoned white American who sometimes affects blackface and who talks variously in the first, second, and third persons. Berryman insisted that this character, "Henry," is not himself, but when Berryman battles alcoholism or breaks his arm, so too does Henry, and Henry's mounting griefs in the sequence are not distinguishable from Berryman's own. *The Dream Songs* (collected in 1969) range freely over many topics and lack the sequential tightness of *Homage to Mistress Bradstreet*, but they are Berryman's most confessional work. His subsequent collections take a more histrionic direction. The poems of *Love & Fame* (1970) and the posthumously published *Delusions, Etc.* (1972) are interesting primarily for their reflection of the author's reactivated Catholicism and for portents of his suicide.

W. D. Snodgrass, Lowell's pupil in the Iowa poetry workshop, was credited by the master with crystallizing self-exposure as a poetic subject. The poems Snodgrass wrote in that workshop were published as *Heart's Needle* (1959) in the same year as *Life Studies*, and they were as critically successful as they proved influential. In ten lyrics that make up the title sequence, Snodgrass details with excruciating candor a father's relation to his three-year-old daughter while he is in the process of divorcing and remarrying. His candor breached formalist decorum all the more successfully because of the conventional formalism of stanza and meter in which it found expression, but the lurking formalism in the collection received as little notice as the bathos that now seems its failing. *After Experience* (1968) continues the confessional disclosures of *Heart's Needle* but with more care to avoid emotional exaggeration. In *The Führer Bunker* (1977), Snodgrass turns away from confessionalism altogether and writes a series of monologues by the various Nazis who surrounded Hitler in his last days, representing

them less as war criminals than as victims of their environment and rearing. It is the most mature and technically brilliant of his collections, although its humanizing of Nazi evil
has raised some hackles.

Anne Sexton was the student of both Lowell and Snodgrass
and more committed to the confessional idiom than either. *To
Bedlam and Part Way Back* (1960), her first collection of poems,
emerged from her initial experiences in a mental hospital, her
agonizing journey "part way back" from insanity, her estrange-
ment from her dying mother and her unfamiliar child. *All My
Pretty Ones* (1962) and *Live or Die* (1966) continued to speak
with terrible candor and unhappiness of a life tortured by a
self-exacerbation that sought release in death. "I was
born/ doing reference work in sin and born/ confessing it," she
wrote. "This is what poems are." The poems of *Transformations*
(1971)—sardonic reworkings of German fairy tales—are the
least confessional of her poems and the most controlled. After
Transformations, she was increasingly unable to shape the
verse that exfoliated from her unhappiness. With few excep-
tions, the poems in *The Death Notebooks* (1974) and the posthumously published collection *The Awful Rowing toward God*
(1975) are the incoherent cries of an anguish that found rest
not in aesthetic closure but in suicide.

Extravagant in its intensities and feverish in its maso-
chistic self-loathing, the poetry of Sylvia Plath passes beyond
the confessional to dithyrambic madness. *The Colossus* (1960),
the single collection published during her lifetime, only begins
to tap the raw power of the poems that were written in the last
months before her suicide and published posthumously in *Ariel*
(1965), *Crossing the Water* (1971), and *Winter Trees* (1971).
Even more painfully than Lowell and Sexton, she is wracked
in that last outpouring by her loneliness, her insecurity, and
her longing for annihilation. Yet she cultivates a range of
voices, from a girlish lilt to a Transylvanian rasp. Surreal imaginings become a kind of ecstasy in poems like "Daddy," while
the brutal facts of her several attempts at suicide are treated
with offhanded coolness in "Lady Lazarus." Like Lowell, who

was once her teacher, she links her personal madness to public dementia and invokes Dachau and Hiroshima as measures of her mind. But an elliptical and allusive syntax and an oscillation between imagistic artifice and honest disclosure are the more deeply grained measure of her terrible dis-ease.

Self-described as "a poet of raw and brutal self-revelation," Clayton Eshleman evokes both the confessionalists and the Beats—the first in his egocentric monologues and sometimes hallucinatory frames of reference, the second in his conceit of journeying to a mystical land where thought and action coalesce. But Eshleman only plays at Beat and confessional introversion in a poetry essentially public and declamatory. In verses that sprawl disjointedly in more than two dozen small volumes, he pursues an elaborately blazoned course through two marriages, several countries, and the contrarieties of his nature. At its best, his poetry has the primitive strength of a sledgehammer; at its worst, it bludgeons us with Eshleman's pride in living by imagination and experiment.

Sandra Hochman also finds autobiography her essential subject, and like Eshleman she sometimes discourses on the minutiae of her life when she has little to say. But Hochman's poetry is generously endowed with insights broadly applicable to the life of women, and her free verse lyrics in *Voyage Home* (1960), *Manhattan Pastures* (1963), *The Vaudeville Marriage* (1966), *Love Letters from Asia* (1968), and *Futures* (1974) evoke childhood loneliness, motherhood, and relationships with husbands and lovers in a tone of shared intimacy. Founded often in specifically detailed landscapes, her poems shift to inner, more evanescent landscapes—amalgams of fantasy, memory, and reality that disclose unconscious wellsprings. "Dream, and poetry of the unconscious, both have a logic of their own," she remarks. "The role of the poet is not to interfere with that order but to be an instrument through which these concepts flow."

Stanley Plumly's poetry is impressive for its technical precision and polish but most compelling for its autobiographical content. He focuses on the memory of an alcoholic father, a much put-upon mother, and a series of failed marriages, and he attempts to confront his own psychological character through this remembrance of things past. The poems of *In the Outer Dark* (1970) suggest the necessity of his turning from the outer dark of his life to the inner dark—essentially, his need to confront the specter of his father and to resolve the disorder of his feelings. *Giraffe* (1973) extends the scenario to the poet's several attempts at love and marriage, attempts thwarted by his unresolved sonship. In *Out-of-the-Body Travel* (1977), his finest collection of poems, Plumly focuses almost entirely on the two parental figures and seems to distill a kind of resolution when he invokes his father and says, "Be with me when I wake." This continuing saga of Plumly's emotional life is too poised to be credited with confessional passion, but it is the more solidly crafted for its emotional awareness and control.

Marvin Bell is also an autobiographical poet preoccupied with sonship and family, but he brings to these themes a greater range of tone than Plumly. The poems in *A Probable Volume of Dreams* (1969), *The Escape into You* (1971), *Residue of Song* (1974), and *Stars Which See, Stars Which Do Not See* (1977) are variously morose, witty, allusive, intense, comic, expansive—often complexly bittersweet, funny-sad. They are also progressively better as they evolve from a loose confessionalism in some of the earliest poems to epiphanic resolutions and a new range of subjects among the most recent. Although technical ability has been manifest in Bell's poetry from the beginning, he seems now to evidence a new maturity.

There is little suggestion in William Heyen's poetry that he is driven by the confessional impulse, although the bulk of his poetry is occasioned by his experiences growing up on Long Island, his German heritage, and his life now in Brockport, New York. Yet he seems fascinated by the origination of his poems, even to sandwiching long prose memoirs on the subject into *Noise in the Trees* (1974), *The Swastika Poems* (1977), and *Long Island Light* (1979). He likes to probe the jarring elements of his life, not in some psychic frenzy, but in the hope they will settle into harmony. Thus, he juxtaposes village life on Long

Island in the 1940s and the contemporary suburban sprawl, human death and natural disaster. In *The Swastika Poems*, his most interesting collection, he scratches through personal scar tissue and imagines the Nazi uncles he never knew, remembers the painted swastika that appeared one day on his boyhood home, permits himself full realization of the Holocaust as he walks the streets of modern Hanover with his wife and visits the concentration camp at Bergen-Belsen. In the quiet decency of his autobiographical candor, Heyen and poets like him temper the confessional impulse that blazed so whitely in the 1960s. Stepping back, as it were, from the frontiers of madness, they position themselves in the middle distance of the ego, acknowledging their sins, but acknowledging also their self-respect.

THE NEW YORK POETS

The New York poets are the most radically antiformalist of the recent schools of poetry. Influenced greatly by an involvement with European and New York painters, influenced also by the free-verse paragraph in contemporary French poetry, they reject the traditional coherencies of line, syntax, and stanza for modes of presentation more spatial than logical, more textural than ideational. Clarity, argument, and explicability they esteem less than immediacy, open forms, and juxtaposed images. Frank O'Hara (1926–1966), John Ashbery (b. 1927), and Kenneth Koch (b. 1925) formed the original nucleus of the group and remain its most influential craftsmen. Ted Berrigan (b. 1934), Ron Padgett (b. 1942), Barbara Guest (b. 1920), James Schuyler (b. 1923), and Edward Field (b. 1924) are also accounted members.

Little published in his lifetime—unconcerned, in fact, with publication—Frank O'Hara was nevertheless a prolific writer, whose *Collected Poems* (ed. Donald Allen, 1971) runs to more than five hundred pages. Although proficient in the traditional forms of poetry, he wrote primarily improvisational verse. The quick notation of a New York City street scene, the memory of a casual remark, and the rambling account of his days and ways are typical forms of his poetry. Its charm is a train of bright particulars shunted freely from track to track in a transcriptional fidelity to consciousness. Colloquial, witty, sometimes extravagantly fantastical, he brings a quality of attention to mundane reality that makes it seem serendipitous. Much has been made of O'Hara's debt to the surrealists and the dadaists, and to the New York painters Jackson Pollock, Willem de Kooning, and Grace Hartigan, who were his friends. But a poem like "The Day Lady Died" transcends all lines of influence with its insistent parataxis and (literally) breathtaking conclusion.

John Ashbery's ultimate goal appears to be nothing less than the deconstruction of modernism. The elaborate shapings of the modernist poet and his freight of image, symbol, and myth are jettisoned in Ashbery's poetry for an aesthetic of inconsequence, nonstatement, and incompletion. He attempts, he says, "to keep meaningfulness up to the pace of randomness" in his poetry, but it is generally felt that he achieves the random more successfully than the meaningful. Except for a very few poems, the collections *The Tennis Court Oath* (1962), *Rivers and Mountains* (1966), *The Double Dream of Spring* (1970), and *Three Poems* (1972) seem exercises in inclusion, random gatherings that have no issue in awareness or discovery. The poems in *Self-Portrait in a Convex Mirror* (1975) are more accessible, inasmuch as they suggest a sensibility in the act of creating itself as it mirrors the random universe. Alive, shifting, as various as the peaks and pratfalls of life, that self steps forward whenever literary effects threaten to stylize or eclipse it, and it indulges every conceivable distraction. Presumably, the poems in *Houseboat Days* (1977), *As We Know* (1979), and *Shadow Train* (1981) should be read as similar instances of a self-creation attuned to the randomness of life, although such an understanding is difficult to sustain. What distinguishes Ashbery's poetry, despite all obstacles to understanding, is a lapidary texture that rises into deeply sculpted detail and relaxes into finely engraved pictures and emblems. His ability to snare us with the quotidian is matched only by O'Hara.

Kenneth Koch brings a greater sense of literary tradition to his poetry than either O'Hara or Ashbery, and he seems, therefore, more academic than they. But the academic is only an occasion in Koch's poetry for surrealistic capering. He begins his poetic career with a long narrative poem, *Ko; or, A Season on Earth* (1959), which teases the epic tradition by twitching from one story line to another and by amassing a wealth of absurd conceits and inapposite rhymes. In *Thank You, and Other Poems* (1962), he scoffs at poets "gargling out" academic verse with their eyes "on the myth/ And the Missus and the midterms," and in *When the Sun Tries to Go On* (1969) he serves up a poem monstrously prolonged—a travesty of postmodern open-endedness. In more recent collections, such as *The Burning Mystery of Anna in 1951* (1979), Koch has adopted a calmer and more thoughtful tone than before, even a note of melancholy, as if weary of his reputation as a cutup. At the same time, he has gained considerable eminence as a teacher of poetry. Indeed, nothing has done more to convey his seriousness about poetry and its ability to renew the self than his highly regarded treatises about teaching poetry: *Wishes, Lies, and Dreams: Teaching Children to Write Poetry* (1970); *Rose, Where Did You Get That Red?: Teaching Great Poetry to Children* (1973), and *I Never Told Anybody: Teaching Poetry Writing in a Nursing Home* (1977).

Ted Berrigan is more attuned to conventional form than the other New York poets, but in a disruptive, antiformalist way. In *The Sonnets* (1964), his first important collection, he distorts the sonnet form with irregular, unmetered verse, and opens it to the unexpected juxtapositions of collage by systematically dislocating individual lines and passages. Such techniques seem to fascinate Berrigan, and he has continued to experiment with textual disjunction. In *Bean Spasms* (1967), a collaborative venture with Ron Padgett and artist Joe Brainard, whole sections of poems have been shifted about in a manner that recalls the cut-up sentences of William Burroughs.

The collection *In the Early Morning Rain* (1970) contains a similar collaboration in which Berrigan and Dick Gallup (b. 1941) are the authors of alternate lines of the poem "80th Congress." The success of such poetry is equivocal. Like much of the "action" painting that influences it, it seems more a symbolic gesture than a craft.

Much the same point about symbolic gesture is valid for Ron Padgett's poetry. Marked by directionless wordplay and an intensification of the most trivial details, it is a surreal, sometimes dadaistic body of poetry that glistens seductively on the surface but slips often into incoherence. Like Berrigan, Padgett is drawn to collaboration. *Some Things* (1964), an unbound sheaf of fifteen captioned drawings, was produced with Ted Berrigan and Joe Brainard several years before they joined forces again on *Bean Spasms. The Adventures of Mr. & Mrs. Jim and Ron* (1970) and *Oo La La* (1973) are collaborations with the artist Jim Dine, *Back in Boston Again* (1972) a collaboration with Berrigan and Tom Clark (b. 1941). Padgett succeeds best when he injects a note of childish whimsy into his surreal fantasies, and he succeeds least when his gamesmanship is esoteric. "Some Bombs" (1969), a poem in which an incoherent English text is actually a mispronounced French text, is one of the monster poems of modern literature.

Like many of the New York poets, Barbara Guest employs a painterly technique with a fine sense of its applicability to language. In collections such as *The Location of Things* (1960), *The Blue Stairs* (1968), and *Moscow Mansions* (1973), she tends to treat her verbal elements less as conceptual or emotional referents than as line, texture, and color. She disposes these elements in highly personal ways, but there is an inveterate chill to her poetry—a cosmopolitan refinement that supersedes anything truly personal. She is, perhaps, the most elegant of the New York poets, remarkable for the assurance and intelligence of her poetry, remarkable also for her ability to evoke through imagistic montages a sense of psychological dislocation.

James Schuyler is also a painterly poet, concerned more

to arrange his sensations and impressions into abstract shapes than to probe them for larger meanings. He avoids grand truths and dramatic incidents, keeping close to unadorned memory, objects, and sensations, and he avoids symbolic elaborations of the "dirty socks in dirty sneakers" and "capless tubes of unguents" that anchor his poems in the mundane. In the collections *Freely Espousing* (1969), *The Crystal Lithium* (1972), and *Hymn to Life* (1974), he shifts from disjunctive to more tightly organized forms, but evocations of the ordinary remain his most arresting effects. The month of March arrives, he says, "like a granny/ a child doesn't/ like to kiss." "I like it," he says, "when the morning sun lights up my room/ Like a yellow jelly bean."

In his distaste for such traditional disciplines of poetry as rhyme and meter and in his gravitation toward the surreal image, Edward Field aligns himself with the New York poets, although he is less interested than they in orchestrating a perceptual fantasia and more interested in laying bare a surrealism at the heart of apparent coherence. Indeed, he strikes an oracular note in this regard with the poems of *Stand Up, Friend, with Me* (1963) as he struggles to reconcile elemental paradoxes with truths of the common life. He finds his best, most surrealistic material in popular iconography, however, particularly in the products of Hollywood. In the poems of *Variety Photoplays* (1967) he looks beyond the films of Frankenstein, Tarzan, and Joan Crawford to the polymorphous-perverse that he thinks they celebrate. Less exclusively attuned to the verbal surface than the other New York poets, he is more attuned to the existential depths.

DEEP IMAGISTS

Unhappy with the tendency of the New York poets to fragment reality into a discontinuous stream of images, a group of poets known as the deep imagists argue that the most affecting kind of poetry springs from what Jung describes as archetypes of the unconscious and what they call the "deep image." The deep image is a concrete detail that surges up from the poet's unconscious in a context of powerful feelings and re-creates for the reader a lost order of understanding. It is discovered, they assert, by the mind leapfrogging backward over the rational discourse of the subjective ego into a mode of awareness that is unitary, prerational, mythically authoritative, transpersonal. They cluster around two publishing organs: Robert Bly's (b. 1926) journal and press successively entitled *The Fifties*, *The Sixties*, and *The Seventies*, and Robert Kelly's (b. 1935) now-defunct journal entitled *Trobar*. James Wright (1927–1980), Louis Simpson (b. 1923), and James Dickey (b. 1923) have been associated with Bly, Jerome Rothenberg (b. 1931) and Diane Wakoski (b. 1937) with Kelly.

In a relatively small but influential body of poetry, Robert Bly has struggled to accommodate several very different voices: the quiet voice of a man drawn to the deepest, most illumining wellsprings of unconscious life; the hectoring, sometimes caustic voice of a man deeply angered by American institutions; recently, in *The Man in the Black Coat Turns* (1982), a voice darkly somber. *Silence in the Snowy Fields* (1962), his first collection of poems, is made up primarily of tributes to pastoral solitude, but in *The Light around the Body* (1967) and *Sleepers Joining Hands* (1973), he looses a moral outrage oddly uncoordinated with his introversions. "The life of the country," he insists, "can be imagined as a psyche larger than the psyche of anyone living, a larger sphere, floating above everyone." Whatever the propriety of equating the national psyche with Jung's collective unconscious, Bly's political poetry fails to achieve the influence of his meditative verse. For this reason, perhaps, he abandons topical relevance in the collection *This Tree Will Be Here for a Thousand Years* (1979) and turns to a poetry of "two presences"—his own and the consciousness he affects to share with plants and animals. Attracted to irrationalist writers in other cultures, Bly also translates Rilke and García Lorca, the Latin American poets César Vallejo, Pablo Neruda, and Juan Ramón Jiménez, the Austrian poet

Georg Trakl, and the Scandinavian poets Tomas Tranströmer and Gunnar Ekelöf. Ironically, his translations illustrate somewhat better than his original poetry the resonance of the collective unconscious.

Unlike Bly, Robert Kelly is as impressive as a craftsman as he is influential as a theoretician. Craft, he argues, is a "perfected attention" of the whole human organism to images deep in the collective unconscious, and he sees a poem's form and subject matter welling up in this act of attention like Helicon's harmonious spring. Kelly's poems are blendings of the real and the surreal so adroit as to lend credibility to this theory of a poem's origin, notably in the collections *Armed Descent* (1961), *Finding the Measure* (1968), *Kali Yuga* (1970), and *The Convections* (1977). What emerges from these works is a poetry passionately engaged with the whole of human experience— the physical, the intellectual, the spiritual. Freely allusive and improvisational in form, the poems bespeak an imagination unfettered but focused, liberated but ingathering. Eternity, Kelly says in *The Mill of Particulars* (1973), looms beyond the grid of speech.

James Wright's early poems in *The Green Wall* (1957) and *Saint Judas* (1959) are traditionally metered and logically discursive studies of human life gone amiss, poems very much in the tradition of Robinson, Frost, and Roethke. But with *The Branch Will Not Break* (1963) and *Shall We Gather at the River* (1968), the character of Wright's poetry altered. Lines like "I have wasted my life" and "How lonely the dead must be" open sudden chasms of feeling in poems otherwise serene, chasms that stretch downward to the emotional gestalt of the deep image. Description in these poems replaces the deductive structure of the earlier poetry; the non sequitur replaces closure; and the unanswerable question replaces symmetry. During the period he wrote these deeply affecting poems, Wright was also translating the poets Trakl, Vallejo, and Neruda, and their irrationalism seems to have been for him, as for Bly, a stylistic catalyst. His later poetry, collected in *Two Citizens* (1973), *To a Blossoming Pear Tree* (1977), and *This Journey* (1982), is less dependent on sudden openings in the surface of a poem, more dependent on a dreamlike fluidity of emotion and a plain-speaking style. Yet Wright was in both of his mature styles a formidable explorer of human unhappiness. His poems about alienation and the harshness of nature have a psychological probity seldom matched in contemporary American poetry.

Like Wright, Louis Simpson began his career as a traditionalist. The poems in *The Arrivistes* (1949) and *Good News of Death* (1955) are attentive to metrics and rhyme and pay homage to influences as diverse as Auden, the Cavaliers, and the war poets Randall Jarrell and Karl Shapiro. But even in his early collections, Simpson's mix of such influences has a narrative cast entirely his own—most finely achieved, perhaps, in the war poem "Carentan O Carentan." In the collection *At the End of the Open Road* (1963), he began to open his poems to free verse and to dot them with surrealistic images, gracing his narratives with a new emotive power. The influence of Kelly and Bly is evident in the surrealism of these *Open Road* poems, and the influence of Whitman's vision of America is everywhere manifest, but Simpson continues to uphold the traditionalist ideal of "a poetry that addresses itself to the human condition, a poetry of truth, not dreams." In the autobiographical excursions of *Adventures of the Letter I* (1971) and *Searching for the Ox* (1976), he defines himself not by confessionalist fantasy but by reference to his Russian ancestry and Jamaican background.

Although James Dickey disdains identification with all schools of poetry, the irrationalist energy of his poems and his sense of participating in some overarching oneness of time and being link him to the deep imagists. His goal, he says, is "a fusion of inner and outer states, of dream, fantasy, and illusion where everything partakes of the protagonist's mental processes and creates a single impression." In collections such as *Drowning with Others* (1962), *Helmets* (1964), *Buckdancer's Choice* (1965), and *The Eye-Beaters, Blood, Victory, Madness, Buckhead and Mercy* (1970), he achieves this goal by focusing on the bizarre—on a misbegotten sheep-child, a stewardess plunging earthward in an erotic embrace of the air, blind children who beat themselves in the eyes to stimulate nervous sensations approximating sight. Such surreal imaginings seem to express for Dickey a challenging doubleness in the human condition. Indeed, his best poems, such as "Falling," "Drinking from a Helmet," and "The Firebombing," depend on the mismatch of an objective scene and a subjective experience. There is a deliberate formlessness in such poems, but narrative sweep and lurching rhythms convey an energy so atavistically healthy that it transcends equipoise. Recent poems, collected in *The Strength of Fields* (1979), seem less healthy. In their manneredness and constraint, they are evidence that Dickey's most successful mode is the Dionysian.

Jerome Rothenberg is generally credited with coining the phrase *deep image*, but his early poetry, collected in *White Sun Black Sun* (1960) and *The Seven Hells of Jigoku Zoshi* (1962), seem to have exhausted his interest in the isolated deep image. He turned in *Poland/1931* (1970) to a new, more comprehensive tapping of the unconscious. A series of poems that follows the Jewish experience from the European ghettos to the American cities, *Poland/1931* is an attempt to write what Rothenberg terms "ancestral poetry," to reach back "through the terms of a collective unconscious, to the particular terms of a particular people," to (re)create, in short, a tribal rather than a merely individual poetry. Rothenberg has continued to strive for such a poetry in the various editions of his *Seneca Journal* (1973, 1975, 1978), but anthologies of folk literature have proved a more viable means to his end. *Technicians of the Sacred* (1968), *Shaking the Pumpkin* (1972), and *America a Prophesy* (with George Quasha, 1973) are anthologies important for their range of Native American materials and for startling juxtapositions that undercut the presumptions of rationalistic cultures. In *Revolution of the Word* (1974) and *A Big Jewish Book* (1978) Rothenberg steers the same course in new waters, not always with anthropological soundness, but with fascinating bravura.

Diane Wakoski's poetry tends to derive from unhappy private experiences—relationships with men, for the most part—but she moves beyond the autobiographical narrative into the domain of the deep image in her poems based on these experiences. In "Justice Is Reason Enough," a poem in *Coins and Coffins* (1962), the inexplicable suicide of a younger brother finds psychic resolution in a Leda-and-the-Swan incest fantasy. Unable to speak her father's name until "a woodpecker with fresh bloody crest" knocks at her mouth, she identifies the first United States president with both her father and American society in the *George Washington Poems* (1967) and turns an extended meditation on the male sex into surreal autobiography. A precise and unpretentious style, acutely sensuous imagery, and a conscious use of analogically musical forms distinguish Wakoski's recent poetry somewhat more than the shocking image and the surrealistic drift.These qualities are especially notable in *Waiting for the King of Spain* (1976), her most assured and polished collection to date.

BLACK POETS

Like black novelists and dramatists, black poets have tended to assert an ethnic identity in their art—proudly, gravidly, often militantly. Nonblacks are generally warned off the premises. "Black literature is literature BY blacks," says Gwendolyn Brooks, "ABOUT blacks, directed TO blacks." In the 1940s and 1950s, black poetry tended to accommodate itself to the prevailing aesthetic norms, but the Black Power movement in the 1960s spawned a poetry of ethnic pride, sometimes peacockery, which has proven itself more concerned with the social uses of verse than with matters of form and technique. The genius of this poetry tends to be a syntactical rhythm more suited to performance than to the page. Gwendolyn Brooks (b. 1917), Robert Hayden (1913–1980), Amiri Baraka (b. 1934), and Nikki Giovanni (b. 1943) stand out among contemporary black poets; Don L. Lee (b. 1942), Mari Evans (b. 1923), Sonia

Sanchez (b. 1934), and Lucille Clifton (b. 1936) have also earned substantial reputations.

Gwendolyn Brooks's early poems, collected in *A Street in Bronzeville* (1945), *Annie Allen* (1949), and *The Bean Eaters* (1960), are compassionate portraits of impoverished ghetto-dwellers on Chicago's South Side, poems very much in the tradition of her fellow Illinoian Edgar Lee Masters. With the title sequence of *In the Mecca* (1968), Brooks's portraits take on a fiercer tone, becoming emotional polemic. Based narratively on the murder of a black child and the refusal of neighbors in an apartment complex to help the mother when she thinks her daughter lost, the sequence reflects the growing consciousness in the civil rights movement of the link between political oppression, poverty, and human unfeelingness. In the poems of *Riot* (1969), *Family Pictures* (1970), and *Beckonings* (1975), Brooks has continued as a voice of the new black consciousness, but as part of her ongoing commitment to speak both to and for black people, she has tended to replace the ballads and sonnets of her early poetry with flexible forms less associated with the literary traditions of Western Europe. She remains, however, a virtuoso of the lyric and an extraordinary portrait-ist—probably the finest black poet of the post-Harlem generation.

Robert Hayden's work is less well known than Brooks's, partly because it is a relatively small oeuvre, partly because Hayden alienated many of his fellow blacks by his disdain for ethnocentric poetics. He is best represented by his *Selected Poems* (1966) and *Angle of Ascent: New and Selected Poems* (1975)—work grounded in the black experience but luxuriating in verbal patterns and hard-edged structures rather than in sociopolitical commentary. His most interesting work is historical. "Middle Passage" is based partly on the 1839 insurrection aboard the Spanish slave ship *Amistad*; "Runagate, Runagate" is distilled from journals, narratives, and histories dealing with the Underground Railroad; and "El-Hajj Malik El-Shabazz" considers the place in history to be accorded the

Black Muslim leader Malcolm X. Such poems deserve a more general renown than they enjoy, for Hayden's grace of mind and art was considerable.

Associated originally with the Projectivists and the Beats, Amiri Baraka (formerly LeRoi Jones) showed in his early poetry a talent for elliptical verse that seems the natural overflow of a sensibility elementally and self-consciously "hip." Indeed, the poems in *Preface to a Twenty Volume Suicide Note* (1961) suggest a sensibility fulfilled by the freedoms of postmodern art. With the poems of *The Dead Lecturer* (1964), Baraka began to express an intemperate outrage with white America. "Rape the white girls," he enjoins in the sequence "Black Dada Nihilismus"; "Rape/ Their fathers. Cut the mothers' throats." In the subsequent collections *Black Art* (1966), *Black Magic* (1969), *It's Nation Time* (1970), and *Hard Facts* (1975), Baraka transforms his earlier, not-obviously-black poetry into revolutionary diatribe. He has come to rely increasingly on his natural eloquence rather than on studied technique, and he describes his recent productions as "poems that kill," "poems that shoot/ guns." Baraka is not the first, of course, to forge a political weapon from literature. Nor is he the first to lose his literary audience in the process.

Nikki Giovanni shares Baraka's militancy, but her poetry is less programmatically a call to arms than his and more often a personal statement. Pedestrian, half-thought abstractions sap the strength of her work from *Black Feeling, Black Talk* (1968) to *Cotton Candy on a Rainy Day* (1978), but her poems gradually become more narratively and lyrically imaginative, somewhat richer in human feeling. She is her best when she evokes individual blacks—the gangster Harold Logan, the singer Aretha Franklin, the revolutionist Angela Davis—her weakest when she wrenches lines in an attempt to imitate the rhythms of black music. "Perhaps these are not poetic/ times," she muses, but the general thinness of her verse seems due to lack of technical proficiency.

The so-called New Black Aesthetic finds its formal inspiration in jazz and tends to seek a clarity of statement that simplifies the complexity of experience. If the work of Baraka and Giovanni illustrates such a black aesthetic, so too does the work of Don L. Lee. A prolific writer, his poems in such collections as *Think Black* (1967), *Don't Cry, Scream* (1969), and *Directionscore* (1971) are statements of black consciousness first and poetry second. His most interesting work is "Black Sketches," a sequence of eleven short poems in *Don't Cry, Scream*. Ostensibly autobiographical in its discovery of black consciousness, the sequence suggests the coming to consciousness of American blacks in general. Lee can be tedious in the reiteration of his controlling insights, but he is inventive with his visual forms and increasingly skilled with his rhythmic effects. Not the least appeal of his verse is its considerable wit.

Mari Evans has also been successful in accommodating the new black consciousness within poetry that surrenders no measure of its wit and gentle irony to social critique. In the poems of *Where Is All the Music?* (1968) and *I Am a Black Woman* (1970), she asserts racial pride and anchors her feelings firmly in the concrete. Less subtle in her effects, Sonia Sanchez hammers away at a few simple points, often in elaborately inflected black dialect, and in collections such as *We a BaddDDD People* (1970), she unfurls her black pride with an angry disdain for white America and for blacks "in wite powder that removes/ them from they blk/ selves." Lucille Clifton's three collections of poetry, *Good Times* (1969), *Good News about the Earth* (1972), and *An Ordinary Woman* (1974), chart a moving tale of the black expectations raised in the 1960s and tempered in the 1970s. Her poetry is especially notable for its understated technique and for its powerful vignettes about life in the ghetto.

THE INDEPENDENTS

Schools of poetry tend to please literary historians more than poets, for schools are critical conveniences that tend to minimize some of the most interesting differences among writers.

Many contemporary American poets defy alignment with schools and speak in voices neither confessional, Beat, nor deep imagist, neither Black Mountain, New York, nor San Franciscan. The most accomplished of these independents are W. S. Merwin (b. 1927), A. R. Ammons (b. 1926), Galway Kinnell (b. 1927), William Stafford (b. 1914), and Dave Smith (b. 1942). Other independents of note are Michael Benedikt (b. 1935), Brendan Galvin (b. 1938), David Ignatow (b. 1914), Philip Levine (b. 1928), Theodore Weiss (b. 1916), Linda Pastan (b. 1932), Mark Strand (b. 1934), Ann Stanford (b. 1916), and Nancy Willard (b. 1936).

The poetry of W. S. Merwin follows a course of development roughly analogous to the course of postwar American poetry. The poems of *A Mask for Janus* (1952) and *The Dancing Bears* (1954) are written in the neoclassical mode of the 1950s, and their ballads, songs, and odes reach back to ancient myths and heroic motifs in a manner smoothly impersonal. In *The Drunk in the Furnace* (1960) and *The Moving Target* (1963), Merwin roughened his meters and turned to portraiture of himself and his family in such a way as to suggest an influence of Lowell's *Life Studies*. An interest in unconscious forces and surrealistic modes of dislocation in *Writings to an Unfinished Accompaniment* (1973) suggests an influence of the New York poets, although the influences upon Merwin are more credibly European—the aphoristic poetry of René Char, for instance, and the elliptical poetry of Jorge Guillén. In *The Compass Flower* (1977), he cultivates the solipsistic resonance of the deep imagists.

Despite this tendency in his oeuvre to accommodate the reigning modes of poetry, Merwin is in no way a slave of fashion. Every stage of his poetic development emerges out of a previous stage and is a growth by graceful steps toward the ultimate poem that he envisions as a "finality of utterance." There is a manneredness about his poems that sometimes obscures their force—an etiolation that makes them seem more shadow than fire—but Merwin is without question one of the most proficient and spiritually intrepid of contemporary American poets.

A. R. Ammons is like Wallace Stevens in his Romantic impulse to torture the philosophical problem of the One and the Many, but Ammons gives himself more entirely than Stevens to the world of nature, and nature is for him a matter of birds and tidal estuaries as well as a challenge to the priority of mind. Indeed, the evolution of Ammons's poetry from *Expressions of Sea Level* (1963) through *Corson's Inlet* (1965) to *Northfield Poems* (1966) is an incremental adjustment to the external world, a grounding in reality born of careful attention to the "hues, shadings, rises, flowing bends and blends/ of sight." This adjustment to the world continues to inform his poems, from *Uplands* (1970) through *A Coast of Trees* (1981), and it evolves gradually into an appreciation of the tension between the internality of mind and the externality of nature—into a conviction that the tension between the two is an essential dynamic of life. The fascination of Ammons's poetry is his struggle to arrive at these understandings about the relationship between nature and mind. He struggles with the disciplines of perfect awareness, of transcriptional accuracy, of art, strewing his poems with husks of mental and emotional life as he moves inexorably on, staking out some ultimate battlefield of the Romantic sensibility.

Galway Kinnell also gives himself to the world of nature, but he has a more apocalyptic sense than Ammons of the division between inner and outer life. Poems in *What a Kingdom It Was* (1960) and *Flower Herding on Mount Monadnock* (1964) are rife with a sense that humans need to propitiate nature. "I know I live half alive in the world," he avers in "Middle of the Way"; "I know half my life belongs to the wild darkness." In *Body Rags* (1968) he explores that wild darkness more fully than before, and in poems like "The Porcupine" and "The Bear" he imagines entrance into the dark, violent heart of the non-human. Suffering and death are rituals of reconnection with the outer world in the shamanistic logic of these poems, and to become the flame dancing on the woodpile is to pass beyond division into primordial wholeness. In *The Book of Nightmares* (1971), a sequence modeled on Rilke's *Duino Elegies*, Kinnell continues to grapple with human dividedness and to demonstrate a remarkably keen sense of nature, but the bleakness of his earlier poetry is modified as he attends to the cycles of human existence, framing the *Nightmares* sequence with poems on the respective births of his children, striating it with moments of tenderness and humor. In the poems of *Mortal Acts, Mortal Words* (1980), he maintains this new concern with personal and domestic circumstances.

William Stafford also addresses the subject of human separation from the natural world, but from a viewpoint less intense than Kinnell's. *West of Your City* (1960) and five subsequent collections gathered in *Stories That Could Be True* (1977) are characterized by casual, idiomatic, almost daydreaming poems that have their origin in epiphanic moments and seem sacramental acts of intuition. Deeply attentive to both mental and physical space, Stafford is moved by the landscape of the Pacific Northwest, bewitched by memory, consumed by a sense of transcendent unity. "It is all right," he says, "to be simply the way you have to be,/ among contradictory ridges in some crescendo of knowing." The cost of such passivity is a poetry less vigorous than it sometimes needs to be, but when he succeeds, Stafford is an impressive spokesman for a peculiarly American desolation of mind and wilderness.

The poetry of Dave Smith is intensely wrought, with a fine momentum, a sonorous, heavily accented line, and an impulse to get at the ultimate truth of things. Geographic locales give a focus to his collections—Tidewater Virginia in *Bull Island* (1970) and *The Fisherman's Whore* (1974), Virginia and Maryland in *Cumberland Station* (1976), Wyoming and Utah in *Goshawk, Antelope* (1979). But Smith is more than a local colorist, however much his works about landscapes and fishing seem to place him in that tradition. Narrative and oracular strains in his verse emphasize the terrible effacements of shipwreck, sickness, and death, the awesome integrity of building, sailing, and

giving birth. "I love poems which admit me to that private
chapel soul of the soul where things matter," he says, "where
I know what I encounter will make me pay for my life, pay in
self-change." Midway in a career of signal promise, he is one
of the most talented young poets writing in America today.

Michael Benedikt has given free rein to a vigorous talent
that embraces both realism and surrealism, both verse and the
prose poem. Much of his work seems more clever than substantial, but cleverness must be risked when one unleashes
metaphors that link the most improbable bits and pieces of
experience and sets in motion queer allegories that jumble the
human and the nonhuman multiformally. Most of Benedikt's
early poems in *Changes* (1961), *The Body* (1968), and *Sky*
(1970) are just such surrealistic play, and at their best they
are fantasies that tease our self-conscious intelligence and our
fatigued sense of reality. Benedikt's prose poems are also at
their best as surrealistic play. A sequence of prose poems unified by a "mole" consciousness, *Mole Notes* (1971) is the author's preeminent attempt to burrow into the complex amalgam of intellect, imagination, and the material world, but the
prose poems of *Night Cries* (1976) more convincingly evoke
moments of realistic consciousness informed by surreality.

Brendan Galvin is capable of images almost as startling
as Benedikt's, but he prefers effects in his poems more organic
than surrealistic. "The true risk is still in presenting felt
expressions of the way things are," he insists, and in his collections *The Narrow Land* (1971), *The Salt Farm* (1972), *No
Time for Good Reasons* (1974), *The Minutes No One Owns*
(1977), and *Atlantic Flyway* (1980), he reviews the way things
are through a wealth of topical anecdotes and from many an-
gles. His Irish heritage, his children, and his distaste for urban
sprawl are occasional subjects of his poetry, but the coastal area
of New England and its bird life are his special focus. An engaging poet with a relaxed, conversational style, he uses a
ready wit to catch our attention, richer involvements to carry
us deeper into statements of unmannered feeling.

The poems of David Ignatow are attempts to formulate a

satisfactory response to human and social dissolution. The venality of American business, the ideological dismemberments of the Vietnam era, and the *Walpurgisnacht* of the New York subway possess Ignatow like contemporary Furies, impelling him to surrealistic parables in the collections *Say Pardon* (1961) and *Figures of the Human* (1964), to poems of more subtle statement in *Rescue the Dead* (1968), *Facing the Tree* (1975), *Tread the Dark* (1978), and *Whisper to the Earth* (1982). Autobiography is never far from the surface of the Ignat〕w poem, and recent volumes articulate a search for reconciliation with a deceased father and with a son in a mental hospital. They articulate also a looming death wish and an attraction to suicide. Pain is the burden of Ignatow's poetry, but sardonicism protects him from self-pity. In "I'm a Depressed Poem," one of many such poems Ignatow writes about his craft, a poem pulls itself together and mocks the reader with fellow feeling: "I've made you thoughtful and sad and now there are two/ of us," it says—"I think it's fun."

Philip Levine shares with Ignatow an interest in the sordidly realistic scene, but he is less concerned to work out his ethical response than to compel our attention to the victims of Hiroshima, the industrial maw, and political imprisonment. "The charred faces, the eyes/ boarded up, the rubble of innards" are the preoccupations of his best poetry, and he forces us to confront the terrors of our estate in verses half narrative and half portraiture that tend to slip into surrealism as into a natural habitat. The poems of *On the Edge* (1961), *Not This Pig* (1968), and *They Feed They Lion* (1972) evolve from traditional meters to more open, prosaic lines, and in *1933* (1974), *Ashes* (1979), and *One for the Rose* (1981), a larger drift becomes apparent from political complaint to songs of lamentation—to elegiac stanzas not only for the lost selves of human beings but for the lost selves of the poet. Political protest remains Levine's most distinctive note, but the new strain of personalism in his poetry threatens to eclipse that note of protest with an oddly prosaic lyricism.

Theodore Weiss conceives of his craft as "a moving toward conventional form and then a sidestepping," as "building up expectations only to shake them with something else." Combining a respect for poetic tradition with an eclectic appropriation of modernist and postmodern techniques, he forges a poetry elegant in its observances, but as quirky as it is learned. The dramatic monologue best contains his energy, notably in his masterpiece "Caliban Remembers" and in *Gunsight* (1962), a book-length poem that attends to the mind of a wounded soldier as anesthesia erodes his consciousness. *The World before Us: Poems 1950–1970* (1970) suggests that the allusive style of Weiss's early work yields to a more open and intimate style, but *Fireweeds* (1976) and a selection of new poems in *Views and Spectacles* (1979) make clear that a modified traditionalism is still his hallmark.

Linda Pastan has demonstrated a flair for strong little poems, effortless on the surface, but darkly observant of life's difficult moments. Her earliest collection, *A Perfect Circle of Sun* (1971), manifests an interesting sensibility, and *Aspects of Eve* (1975), *The Five Stages of Grief* (1978), and *Waiting for My Life* (1981) manifest a swing toward a melancholic feminism that is one of the more effective expressions of the new awareness. The first of these collections takes its cue from Archibald MacLeish's poem "Eve's Exile," and in poems about love, death, and the difficulty of writing verse, Pastan explores questions of dependence and independence en route to a realization that women have been as ill served by themselves as by men. The poems in *The Five Stages of Grief* are grouped under rubrics of denial, anger, bargaining, depression, and acceptance—stages that characterize a gradual coming to terms with death, through which Pastan chronicles her acceptance of entrapment in marriage. In *Waiting for My Life*, she continues to probe agonies of the domestic experience.

Mark Strand brings to his poems an anguish as great as Sylvia Plath's, but unlike Plath he channels his anguish into lyrics reductive in their diction and bone clean in their style.

Indeed, such collections as *Sleeping with One Eye Open* (1964), *Reasons for Moving* (1968), *The Story of Our Lives* (1973), and *The Late Hour* (1978) are characterized by stark and desolate statements of an ego that feels itself bereft of substantial self-hood. Strand perceives a Heideggerian nothingness veiling the true self from a nonself that we inexplicably experience as our being. "In a field/ I am the absence/ of field," he writes in "Keeping Things Whole." "I am what is missing." The beauty of his poems is like that of the desert—arid, austere, a skeletonized landscape of spiritual impasse. It has the subtle tonality and vigorous architecture of ravaged sand and rock, but, like the desert, it is basically monochromatic and can seem unrelieved.

The proliferation and variety of interesting American poets seems to be restrained only by the economics of the publishing industry. In three important collections of her poetry, *The Weathercock* (1966), *The Descent* (1970), and *In Mediterranean Air* (1977), Ann Stanford has demonstrated a mastery of the quiet, unassuming, even exquisite lyric. Nancy Willard's poems in such fine collections as *Skin of Grace* (1967) and *Carpenter of the Sun* (1974) turn minutiae of domestic life into resonant emblems of general human experience. A further list of writers who bring distinction to postwar American poetry should include Stephen Berg (b. 1934), Wendell Berry (b. 1934), Michael Casey (b. 1947), Stephen Dobyns (b. 1941), Carolyn Forché (b. 1950), Marilyn Hacker (b. 1942), John Haines (b. 1924), Andrew Hoyem (b. 1935), Bill Knott (b. 1927), Larry Levis (b. 1946), John Logan (b. 1923), Judith Moffett (b. 1942), Raymond R. Patterson (b. 1929), John Peck (b. 1941), Primus St. John (b. 1939), James Tate (b. 1943), Lewis Turco (b. 1934), Peter Wild (b. 1940), and C. K. Williams (b. 1936).

AFTERWORD

There can be no conclusion to this or any survey of contemporary American literature, because the literature itself does not conclude. The overlapping and mutual interaction of schools and the pluralism of styles in the period are a source of strength here, a source of individuation there, but together they make up a richness not yet simplified in our awareness into a literary gestalt. The term *postmodern*, which has had to serve so often as a tag in these pages, is really an antitag that defers to modernism as if literary character climaxed between 1890 and 1930. *Surrealism*, which has also haunted these pages, offers a similar problem in reference. Our necessary recourse to such terms suggests that postwar American literature does not shape itself into a coherent period independent of modernism—that this survey is necessarily an interim report.

What, in summary, can be reported? In terms of fiction: that ethnicity is locked into a quarrel with metafiction, each profiteering from raids on the other, but each maintaining a distinct character and audience; that ethnicity and fantasy signal a general inability of the narrative imagination to speak more broadly to the human condition. In terms of drama: that a return to ritual, mime, and gesture continues to invigorate the theater but in too great an isolation from centuries of theatrical sophistication; that the runaway economics of theatrical production continues to tap the well-made play and to exact a toll from creativity. In terms of poetry: that improvisational structure is the inescapable drift; that private, confessional, and arcane modes of statement are falling into disrepute as poetry struggles to speak more simply to a larger audience.

The general incoherence of the age makes this unresolved picture inevitable. Contemporary American literature is engaged in selecting and rescuing the urgencies of a variegated national experience that withholds its final metaphor. If its energies seem scattered and its vision seems multilensed, our literature merits respect for its willingness to discover all levels of experience, to bring hidden selves into play, and to allow the energies of art to flow outward into the world. As bold as it is various, it is constrained neither by the experiences art has already mastered nor by experiences as yet unnamed.

SELECTED BIBLIOGRAPHY

Bibliographies

Contemporary Authors: A Bio-Bibliographical Guide to Current Authors and Their Works. Detroit: Gale, 1962–present.

MLA International Bibliography of Books and Articles on the Modern Languages and Literatures. New York: Modern Language Association of America, 1921–present.

Somer, John, and Cooper, Barbara Eck. *American & British Literature 1945–1975: An Annotated Bibliography of Contemporary Scholarship*. Lawrence: Regents Press of Kansas, 1980.

General Studies

Bergman, Ronald. *America in the Sixties: An Intellectual History*. New York: Free Press, 1968.

Berthoff, Warner. *A Literature without Qualities: American Writing since 1945*. Berkeley: University of California Press, 1979.

Cook, Bruce. *The Beat Generation*. New York: Scribners, 1971.

French, Warren, ed. *The Fifties: Fiction, Poetry, Drama*. Deland, Fla.: Everett/Edwards, 1970.

Hassan, Ihab. *Contemporary American Literature, 1945–1972: An Introduction*. New York: Ungar, 1973.

Hoffman, Daniel, ed. *Harvard Guide to Contemporary Writing*. Cambridge, Mass.: Harvard University Press, 1979.

Kazin, Alfred. *Contemporaries*. Boston: Little, Brown, 1962.
Kostelanetz, Richard, ed. *On Contemporary Literature: An Anthology of Critical Essays on the Major Movements and Writers of Contemporary Literature*. New York: Avon, 1964.
———. *The Young American Writers: Fiction, Poetry, Drama, and Criticism*. New York: Funk & Wagnalls, 1967.
Podhoretz, Norman. *Doings and Undoings: The Fifties and After in American Writing*. New York: Farrar, Straus, 1964.
Tytell, John. *Naked Angels: The Lives and Literature of the Beat Generation*. New York: McGraw-Hill, 1976.

Contemporary Fiction

Aldridge, John W. *Time to Murder and Create: The Contemporary Novel in Crisis*. New York: McKay, 1966.
Allen, Mary. *The Necessary Blankness: Women in Major American Fiction of the Sixties*. Urbana: University of Illinois Press, 1976.
Baumbach, Jonathan. *The Landscape of Nightmare: Studies in the Contemporary American Novel*. New York: New York University Press, 1965.
Bryant, Jerry H. *The Open Decision: The Contemporary American Novel and Its Intellectual Background*. New York: Free Press, 1970.
Cope, Jackson I., and Green, Geoffrey. *Novel vs. Fiction: The Contemporary Reformation*. New York: Penguin Books, 1982.
Core, George, ed. *Southern Fiction Today: Renascence and Beyond*. Athens: University of Georgia Press, 1969.
Eisinger, Chester E. *Fiction of the Forties*. Chicago: University of Chicago Press, 1963.
Federman, Raymond, ed. *Surfiction: Fiction Now and Tomorrow*. Chicago: Swallow, 1975.
Harris, Charles B. *Contemporary American Novelists of the Absurd*. New Haven, Conn.: College and University Press, 1971.
Hassan, Ihab. *Radical Innocence: Studies in the Contemporary American Novel*. Princeton, N.J.: Princeton University Press, 1961.
Helterman, Jeffrey, and Layman, Richard, eds. *American Novelists since World War II. Dictionary of Literary Biography*, vols. 2 and 6. Detroit: Gale, 1978, 1980.

Hendin, Josephine. *Vulnerable People: A View of American Fiction since 1945.* New York: Oxford University Press, 1978.

Hollowell, John. *Fact & Fiction: The New Journalism and the Nonfiction Novel.* Chapel Hill: University of North Carolina Press, 1977.

Kazin, Alfred. *Bright Book of Life: American Novelists and Storytellers from Hemingway to Mailer.* Boston: Atlantic/Little, Brown, 1973.

Kennard, Jean E. *Number and Nightmare: Forms of Fantasy in Contemporary Fiction.* Hamden, Conn.: Archon, 1975.

Klein, Marcus. *After Alienation: American Novels in Mid-Century.* Cleveland: World, 1964.

———, ed. *The American Novel since World War II.* Greenwich, Conn.: Fawcett, 1969.

Klinkowitz, Jerome. *Literary Disruptions: The Making of a Post-Contemporary American Fiction.* Urbana: University of Illinois Press, 1975.

Madden, David, ed. *American Dreams, American Nightmares.* Carbondale: Southern Illinois University Press, 1970.

Malin, Irving. *New American Gothic.* Carbondale: Southern Illinois University Press, 1962.

Moore, Harry T., ed. *Contemporary American Novelists.* Carbondale: Southern Illinois University Press, 1964.

Olderman, Raymond M. *Beyond the Waste Land: A Study of the American Novel in the Nineteen-Sixties.* New Haven, Conn.: Yale University Press, 1972.

Pinsker, Sanford. *The Schlemiel as Metaphor: Studies in the Yiddish and American Jewish Novel.* Carbondale: Southern Illinois University Press, 1971.

Rosenblatt, Roger. *Black Fiction.* Cambridge, Mass.: Harvard University Press, 1974.

Rubin, Louis D. *The Faraway Country: Writers in the Modern South.* Seattle: University of Washington Press, 1963.

Scholes, Robert. *Fabulation and Metafiction.* Urbana: University of Illinois Press, 1979.

———. *The Fabulators.* New York: Oxford University Press, 1967.

Schulz, Max F. *Black Humor Fiction of the Sixties: A Pluralistic Definition of Man and His World.* Athens: Ohio University Press, 1973.

———. *Radical Sophistication: Studies in Contemporary Jewish-American Novelists.* Athens: Ohio University Press, 1969.

Stevick, Philip. *Alternative Pleasures: Postrealist Fiction and the Tradition.* Urbana: University of Illinois Press, 1981.

Tanner, Tony. *City of Words: American Fiction, 1950–1970.* New York: Harper & Row, 1971.

Tuttleton, James W. *The Novel of Manners in America.* Chapel Hill: University of North Carolina Press, 1972.

Waldmeir, Joseph J., ed. *Recent American Fiction: Some Critical Views.* Boston: Houghton Mifflin, 1963.

Wallace, Ronald. *The Last Laugh: Form and Affirmation in the Contemporary American Novel.* Columbia: University of Missouri Press, 1979.

Contemporary Drama

Berkowitz, Gerald M. *New Broadways: Theatre across America 1950–1980.* Totowa, N.J.: Rowman and Littlefield, 1982.

Bernstein, Samuel J. *The Strands Entwined: A New Direction in American Drama.* Boston: Northeastern University Press, 1980.

Brustein, Robert. *Critical Moments: Reflections on Theatre and Society, 1973–1979.* New York: Random House, 1980.

――――. *The Culture Watch: Essays on Theatre and Society, 1969–1974.* New York: Knopf, 1975.

――――. *Seasons of Discontent: Dramatic Opinions, 1959–1965.* New York: Simon & Schuster, 1965.

――――. *The Third Theatre.* New York: Knopf, 1969.

Driver, Tom F. *Romantic Quest and Modern Query: A History of the Modern Theatre.* New York: Delacorte, 1970.

Esslin, Martin. *The Theatre of the Absurd.* 3rd ed. London: Methuen, 1974.

Gassner, John. *Theatre at the Crossroads: Plays and Playwrights of the Mid-Century American Stage.* New York: Holt, Rinehart & Winston, 1960.

Gould, Jean. *Modern American Playwrights.* New York: Dodd, Mead, 1966.

Harrison, Paul Carter. *The Drama of Nommo.* New York: Grove, 1972.

Hughes, Catharine. *Plays, Politics, and Polemics.* New York: Drama Book Specialists/Publishers, 1973.

Kernan, Alvin B., ed. *The Modern American Theater.* Englewood Cliffs, N.J.: Prentice-Hall, 1967.

Lahr, John. *Astonish Me.* New York: Viking, 1973.

————. *Up against the Fourth Wall*. New York: Grove, 1970.

Lewis, Allan. *American Plays and Playwrights of the Contemporary Theatre*. Rev. ed. New York: Crown, 1970.

Little, Stuart W. *Off-Broadway: The Prophetic Theater*. New York: Coward, McCann & Geoghegan, 1972.

Lumley, Frederick. *New Trends in 20th Century Drama*. New York: Oxford University Press, 1972.

MacNicholas, John, ed. *Twentieth-Century American Dramatists. Dictionary of Literary Biography*, vol. 7. Detroit: Gale, 1981.

Mordden, Ethan. *The American Theatre*. New York: Oxford University Press, 1981.

Price, Julia S. *The Off-Broadway Theater*. New York: Scarecrow, 1962.

Salem, James M. *American Drama, 1909–1969*. 2nd ed. Metuchen, N.J.: Scarecrow, 1973.

Weales, Gerald C. *American Drama since World War II*. New York: Harcourt, Brace & World, 1962.

Zeigler, Joseph Wesley. *Regional Theatre: The Revolutionary Stage*. Minneapolis: University of Minnesota Press, 1973.

Contemporary Poetry

Allen, Donald M., and Tallman, Warren, eds. *Poetics of the New American Poetry*. New York: Grove, 1974.

Altieri, Charles. *Enlarging the Temple: New Directions in American Poetry during the 1960s*. Lewisburg, Pa.: Bucknell University Press, 1979.

Boyars, Robert, ed. *Contemporary Poetry in America*. New York: Schocken, 1974.

Charters, Samuel. *Some Poems/Poets: Studies in American Underground Poetry since 1945*. Berkeley, Cal.: Oyez, 1971.

Dickey, James. *Babel to Byzantium: Poets & Poetry Now*. New York: Farrar, Straus & Giroux, 1968.

Gibson, Donald B., ed. *Modern Black Poets: A Collection of Critical Essays*. Englewood Cliffs, N.J.: Prentice-Hall, 1973.

Greiner, Donald J., ed. *American Poets since Word War II. Dictionary of Literary Biography*, vol. 5. Detroit: Gale, 1980.

Henderson, Stephen, ed. *Understanding the New Black Poetry*. New York: William Morrow, 1973.

Heyen, William, ed. *American Poets in 1976*. Indianapolis, Ind.: Bobbs-Merrill, 1976.

Hollander, John, ed. *Modern Poetry: Essays in Criticism*. New York: Oxford University Press, 1968.

Howard, Richard. *Alone with America: Essays on the Art of Poetry in the United States since 1950*. New York: Atheneum, 1969.

Lacey, Paul A. *The Inner War: Forms and Themes in Recent American Poetry*. Philadelphia: Fortress, 1972.

Lieberman, Laurence. *Unassigned Frequencies: American Poetry in Review, 1964–74*. Urbana: University of Illinois Press, 1977.

Malkoff, Karl. *Crowell's Handbook of Contemporary American Poetry*. New York: Crowell, 1973.

———. *Escape from the Self: A Study in Contemporary American Poetry and Poetics*. New York: Columbia University Press, 1977.

Mazarro, J., ed. *Modern American Poets*. New York: McKay, 1970.

Mersmann, James F. *Out of the Vietnam Vortex: A Study of Poets and Poetry against the War*. Lawrence: University Press of Kansas, 1974.

Mills, Ralph J., Jr. *Contemporary American Poetry*. New York: Random House, 1965.

———. *Cry of the Human: Essays on Contemporary American Poetry*. Urbana: University of Illinois Press, 1975.

Molesworth, Charles. *The Fierce Embrace: A Study of Contemporary American Poetry*. Columbia: University of Missouri Press, 1979.

Phillips, Robert. *The Confessional Poets*. Carbondale: Southern Illinois University Press, 1973.

Pinsky, Robert. *The Situation in Poetry: Contemporary Poetry and Its Tradition*. Princeton, N.J.: Princeton University Press, 1976.

Poulin, A., Jr., ed. *Contemporary American Poetry*. Boston: Houghton Mifflin, 1971.

Rosenthal, M. L. *The New Poets: American and British Poetry since World War II*. New York: Oxford University Press, 1967.

Shaw, Robert B., ed. *American Poets since 1960: Some Critical Perspectives*. Cheadle, England: Carcanet, 1973.

Stepanchev, Stephen. *American Poetry since 1945: A Critical Survey*. New York: Harper & Row, 1965.

Vendler, Helen. *Part of Nature, Part of Us: Modern American Poets*. Cambridge, Mass.: Harvard University Press, 1980.

INDEX OF NAMES, GENRES, AND MOVEMENTS